I0120013

BURNING DIAGRAMS IN ANTHROPOLOGY

BEFORE YOU START TO READ THIS BOOK, take this moment to think about making a donation to punctum books, an independent non-profit press,

@ https://punctumbooks.com/support/

If you're reading the e-book, you can click on the image below to go directly to our donations site. Any amount, no matter the size, is appreciated and will help us to keep our ship of fools afloat. Contributions from dedicated readers will also help us to keep our commons open and to cultivate new work that can't find a welcoming port elsewhere. Our adventure is not possible without your support.

Vive la Open Access.

Fig. 1. Detail from Hieronymus Bosch, *Ship of Fools* (1490–1500)

BURNING DIAGRAMS IN ANTHROPOLOGY: AN INVERSE MUSEUM. Copyright ©
2024 by Tristan Partridge. This work carries a Creative Commons BY-NC-SA 4.0
International license, which means that you are free to copy and redistribute
the material in any medium or format, and you may also remix, transform, and
build upon the material, as long as you clearly attribute the work to the author
(but not in a way that suggests the author or punctum books endorses you and
your work), you do not use this work for commercial gain in any form whatso-
ever, and that for any remixing and transformation, you distribute your rebuild
under the same license. http://creativecommons.org/licenses/by-nc-sa/4.0/

First published in 2024 by dead letter office, BABEL Working Group, an imprint
of punctum books, Earth, Milky Way.
https://punctumbooks.com

The BABEL Working Group is a collective and desiring-assemblage of schol-
ar–vagabonds with no leaders or followers, no top and no bottom, and only a
middle. BABEL roams and stalks the ruins of the post-historical university as a
multiplicity, a pack, looking for other roaming packs with which to cohabit and
build temporary shelters for intellectual vagabonds. BABEL is an experiment in
ephemerality. Find us if you can.

ISBN-13: 978-1-68571-174-0 (print)
ISBN-13: 978-1-68571-175-7 (ePDF)

DOI: 10.53288/468.1.00

LCCN: 2024945546
Library of Congress Cataloging Data is available from the Library of Congress

Editing: SAJ and Eileen A. Fradenburg Joy
Book design: Hatim Eujayl
Cover design: Vincent W.J. van Gerven Oei

punctumbooks

spontaneous acts of scholarly combustion

HIC SVNT MONSTRA

Tristan Partridge

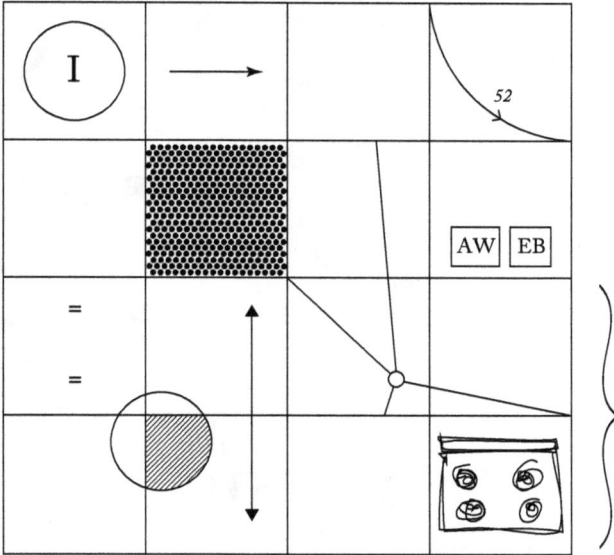

Burning Diagrams in Anthropology

An Inverse Museum

Contents

Acknowledgments

The gratitude I feel for the support and friendship I've received throughout this project, inevitably, exceeds these formal dimensions. Nonetheless, to begin, I want to sincerely thank Alice Street, Jamie Cross, and everyone involved in the UK ESRC-funded research project "Off The Grid: Relational Infrastructures for Fragile Futures (2013–2015)," including participants in the "Ethnograms" micro-residency held at Edinburgh's Dovecot Studios in 2014. This book grew out of those collective engagements—reckoning with the fraught histories of diagrams in anthropology while also exploring potential futures for (re)visualizing social worlds and relationships.

Many others have accompanied me at key moments in the process of finalizing this work. For their different forms of guidance, inspiration, and timely interventions, I want to thank friends and colleagues who are working variously within, despite, adjacent to, or in dialogue with anthropology: Justin Kenrick, Julie Maldonado, Arturo Escobar, Francesca Bray, Maya Mayblin, Magnus Course, Barbara Herr Harthorn, Jane Guyer, Bhrigupati Singh, Dave Novak, Casey Walsh, Charlie Hale, Jéssica Malinalli Coyotecatl Contreras, Ingrid Feeney, Cymene Howe, Gaia von Hatzfeldt, Lucy Lowe, Sian Lazar, Casey High, Siobhan Magee, Penny Harvey, Mario Blaser, Poppy Kohner, David Harvey, Jeremy Rayner, Caroline Gatt, Marc Becker, Joe Webster, Stewart Allen, Koreen Reece, Evangelos Chrysagis, Anna Willow, Dana Powell, and Stephanie Loveless, together with everyone else whose input and influence I have benefited from in the department of Social Anthropology at the University of Edinburgh, throughout the Scottish Training in Anthropological Research network, at the Escuela de Antropología de la Pontificia Universidad Católica de Chile, at ICTA-Barcelona, and at the University of California, Santa Barbara.

There are many dear friends whose writing and visual work continue to illuminate my path: thank you to Iain Findlay-Walsh, Calum Penelope Davidson, Alasdair Raga Campbell, Clare Simpson, FK Alexander, Stewart Morgan Hajdukiewicz, Graeme Green, David Pellow, Sam Wiseman, Luke Matthews, Du Yun, Khyam Allami, Jeff Thomasson, and Sofía Avila. Thanks also to Eileen, Vincent, Lily, Livy, SAJ, Hatim, and everyone at punctum books, as well as our fellow participants in the author group gatherings — it is a delight to be in community with you.

Time spent in Berlin with Javiera Barandiarán and other American Academy fellows in 2022 was invaluable for drawing together threads of different kinds—thank you, everyone. I am especially grateful to Ariella Azoulay for her generosity and the indelible influence of her multi-faceted work and commitment. And, to end at the beginning, I owe eternal thanks to everyone I have connected with during different moments of my own work in social anthropology—even though this current book project exists and operates within a very distinct space and web of relationships. Thank you to Porfirio Allauca and the whole family, Myriam Allauca, Tannia Rojas, and everyone in San Isidro; to Hema'ny Molina and the Selk'nam community Covadonga Ona; and to Bharat Dogra, Dr. Anupam Bhandari, Seema Panwar Bhandari, and everyone I know in Uttarakhand. It is an absolute honor to count you as friends.

I

An Inverse Introduction

Preface: Extricate: Questions

They have been here since the beginning. They are still here.

Ghosts, regularly summoned, to show readers what someone is thinking. What someone has seen.

Not fictive, not mere apparitions. These ciphers are real. They are present, problematic, and burdened with the will of their creators.

Figures, given new shapes and new purposes in order to continue their work.

The work of haunting the canon, an unfinished endeavor.

The canon, in turn, differentially haunts us all: writers, readers, practitioners, friends, accomplices, interlocutors, subjects, objects, the living, and the dead.

Diagrams, beheld.

Colonial relics refashioned. Reprogrammed for contemporary ends. Unwelcome reminders. Evocative shorthand, reductive gloss. Two dimensions, perhaps two too many?

Or, counterpoint: an avenue of expression that is under-examined and under-explored.

Sensorial, complex. So much potential.

Why Diagrams?

Diagrams in anthropology are anomalous. The discipline has a long history of incorporating visual components — such as photography, cartography, and film — and many anthropologists have contributed to broader debates about visual methods by subjecting these components to significant critical scrutiny. Diagrams, however, have received far less reflexive attention. Theirs is a realm of unanswered questions, neglected critique. Perhaps they have escaped scrutiny since they are periodically peripheral, forgotten about. But they re-emerge, time and again.

Their persistence warrants attention.

Given the longevity of diagrams, studying them is a way to engage with the disciplinary history of anthropology itself — a contested, constructed, fragmented confluence of chronologies.

Questioning the purpose and relevance of diagrams is, likewise, to question the discipline as a whole.

Using diagrams as visual metaphors in anthropology is an established practice. For over a century (at some points more regularly than others), diagrams have appeared among ethnographic texts variously showing the relations, mechanisms, or interactions at play within an area or action of analysis, relaying ideas and observations. In these appearances, diagrams can take on multiple roles: the diagram as method, as representational technique, as conceptual tool.

Diagrams are knowledge devices. They carry cross-cutting ethical, aesthetic, epistemological, and political implications. Analyzing these multiple characteristics and implications means (re)assessing processes of knowledge creation: what kinds of knowledge are being created, by and for who, by what means, and to what ends? This means (re)connecting with a central goal in Linda Tuhiwai Smith's work in *Decolonizing Methodologies*. An imperative shared across knowledge creation contexts: to scrutinize the conditions, tools, and assumptions that shape research design and practices as well as their consequences for research participants and their communities (Smith 1999, ix). A decolonizing and decolonized anthropology actively works toward the empowerment of the people whose lives are being studied and described (Harrison 1997, 5). These objectives — still more evident in the rhetoric of institutions than in their responses to collective action — remain difficult or even nonviable until Land Back demands are met, until meaningful material and systemic changes are achieved, and until diverse global demands for Indigenous nationhood, peoplehood, sovereignty, and autonomy are not only acknowledged but implemented and upheld (Simpson 2014; Durrani 2019; Pasternak, King, and Yesno 2019; Liboiron 2021). Any self-affirming scholarly or institutional embrace of the value of detached critique will necessarily be humbled and de-centered within collective struggle. Paraphrasing Ariella Aïsha Azoulay (2019), it is not possible to decolonize anthropology without decolonizing the world (Fanon 1963; Tuck and Yang 2012). These remain the goals. Unless the visual impact and potential of diagrams can be orchestrated to better achieve these fraught and complex ends, then diagrams in anthropology are already redundant.

More than mere relics, diagrams are ruins. Their date of origin may commonly lie in the past but they continue to impose an active influence on contemporary thinking. Many formal norms — kinship maps where binary men have three sides, women are circles — persist from an era when anthropology was even more explicitly defined by its scientistic (and reductive) ambitions, by an adherence to racism, imperial dogma, and colonial violence, with fewer dissenting voices among its proponents than today. Diagrams project an assumed neutrality, part of a broader intellectual tradition that further silences marginalized groups in service of the assumed authority of Western philosophy, aesthetics, and social theory (Jackson 2002, 72–73). Such projections and ambitions contribute directly to the constitutive logics of colonial thinking, institutions, legacies, and relations (Bonilla 2015). They constitute models of, and models for, control. Revisiting diagrams in anthropology means reconsidering what it is to live among, and work with, such canonical ruins.

The *ruins of empire* are not remnant structures or desolate artifacts, they are political dynamics that differentially shape the present (Gordillo 2013). Such ruins are not merely *found* in imperial projects and in persistent structures of domination. Rather, they are *made* (and continually remade) in the acts of those who benefit from racialized relations of inequality (Stoler 2008). Rejecting ruins, along with their tendency to constrict agency, to negate hope, to curtail imagination, is thus an act of reclamation. If we are to create and embrace opportunities to think and be otherwise — and to instigate the collapse of racialized structures of oppression — then certain ruins are going to have to burn.

Why Burn?

Reflecting on experiences of climate chaos in the USA in 2019, Ryan Cecil Jobson applied to anthropology the critiques of Mike Davis's essay, "The Case for Letting Malibu Burn," which skewers "the colonial temporality of a Lockean liberalism" underpinning nouveau riche fantasies of the enclosure and conquest of nature (Jobson 2020, 261; Davis 1999). Davis's conclusion is to stop constructing evermore resource-intensive forms of defense against the flames and instead to acknowledge the flows of local fire ecologies. That is: to let the Malibu mansions burn.

However, engaging the work of Tyson (2019) on intellectual fatalism, Jobson cautions that the parallel act of letting anthropology burn does not mean abandoning the work of social and cultural criticism in favor of a "scholarly professional fatalism that masquerades as politics" (Jobson 2020, 261). Letting anthropology burn instead entails a call "to abandon its liberal suppositions"; to trouble "inherited colonial geographies" and instead "reanimate ethnographic sites as permeable ecological archives"; to refuse a "fictive separation" of anthropology from the "formalization of the human sciences"; and to reject "ritual self-flagellation" when it seeks to authorize an imagined return to post-crisis "academic normalcy" (Jobson 2020, 260–63). At root, this is what burning anthropology means: abandoning the discipline's discourse of "moral perfectibility" founded in histories of settler colonialism and chattel slavery, liberal humanism, and routinized "ethnographic sentimentalism." Letting anthropology burn in these ways would enable us to imagine a future for the discipline that is "unmoored from its classical objects and referents" (Jobson 2020, 261). Diagrams are among these foundational objects, referents, and ruins. Burning diagrams in anthropology could be a great place to start.

What do we choose to discard, and what do we want to reinvigorate? Davis (1999) argued that local fire ecologies will remove unwieldy, elite, dominant constructions from the Malibu hills. These monuments are disconnected from the Earth relations that sustain that particular place. Erected without need, they are a conspicuous indulgence to inflate the ego of ownership. At the same time, those same flames are a cyclical influence that fosters conditions of vitality for certain plant life and other related beings in the region. Those whose existence and well-being is generated and sustained through placed-based relations — the products and producers of mutuality, symbiosis, and reciprocity. This is the influence for figuratively burning diagrams in anthropology: rejecting the enabled, persistent presence of incongruous constructions and re-centering practice on openness and humility.

This collection does not attempt to complete an historical catalogue of diagrams in anthropology. Nor does it presume to categorize diagrams in order to identify those to be figuratively burned, those to be saved. Such goals are senseless and impossible. There is no erasing the past. It is even more impossible to simply imagine scholarly communities have "moved on" and are safely disconnected from the movements and institutions from which they emerged.

You can't just burn it all to the ground and be done with it. No one gets to simply walk away.

Everyone who *was* implicated is *still* implicated, even after the flames.

No matter how its practitioners position themselves, anthropology is "co-constitutive" of the hierarchies and broader power dynamics that shape practices and societies (Rosa and Bonilla 2017, 203). Critique provides no easy escape. The tendency to "move on" usually means absolution which is a failure to confront everything that hasn't changed, to fully address all the remains that remain intact.

And, besides, what's really left among the ashes and rubble?

A critical and reflexive anthropology cannot rest with figurative acts of *burning*. Such acts might remain merely "the self-indulgent condemnation of traditional techniques and tropes"; more fundamentally what is needed is a radical reappraisal of the "symbolic organization upon which anthropological discourse is premised" (Trouillot 2003, 9). Still, figurative acts of burning can also become acts of refusal. Acts of remembering, not denying. Of refusing adherence to disciplinary normalcy. Igniting to expose. Refusing to allow past crimes to be effectively "sealed" in the past without also collectively taking responsibility for that disciplinary past — acts that recognize the so-called ghosts of the past and their creators as real perpetrators, telling stories in order to "prepare the ground for the reparation of imperial crimes" (Azoulay 2019, 379). Burning to prepare the ground, as the Malibu fire ecologies would teach us. How to enact this, how to embody such a revitalizing approach to change? What would it take to make anthropological work that is "unmoored" from diagrams as classical objects, tropes, and referents?

An Inverse Museum?

The collection matters less than reactions to it.

The images assembled and annotated here form a collection that is partial, fragmented, and incomplete. Intentionally so.

Diagrams are more than just a focal point within written research, and more than outmoded relics still frequently on display. Diagrams also create a window through which to view broader anthropological concerns.

What is being replicated here? And how?

The history of anthropology is a problem. It is perhaps *the* problem for those concerned with its many implications. As

Llobera writes, the fixation on genealogies and genealogies-as-ideologies — together with the pretense that genealogies map actual connections — has created a situation in which disciplinary histories are not explained but rather written in order to justify the "structure of the present" (Llobera 1976, 24). The process is self-reinforcing. Canon setting becomes an "education of attention" — attentive primarily to familiar landmarks and disciplinary standards, the focus is predefined (Gibson 1986). The classics are a distraction, taking up space. Any canon shines light on repeated selections. Compiling a history — or histories — of the discipline's classical referents and identifiable tropes arguably serves only to deepen this recurrent problem.

> Don't lean on a canon where none exists…
> don't reify a canon simply to have one. (Stone 2002, 342)

The anthropological canon is a narrow construct, shaped and reinforced through particular notions of time. Like most canons, it has emerged through processes of habit and violence. Its advocates, not always unwittingly, occupy a self-described center and regard anti-racist, anticolonial, and anti-imperialist struggle as peripheral (Harrison 1988). The canon feeds itself. The discursive field that generates and sustains anthropology as a discipline is the West's "geography of imagination" that categorizes according to its own logics of power and which monopolizes the right to historicity, bolstered by its own form of "monumentalism" for the "myth of an unquestioned Western canon" (Trouillot 2003, 9–10). Assembling and annotating the diagrams collected here is to exhume such myths; to expose the ruins to light; to reassess anthropological involvement with such traditions and visual tools.

Disciplines discipline. They categorize. They filter and rank (Trouillot 2003). They are collectively made and remade by people who act in their name, who carry the flags. States of activity, disciplines police their borders. Together, those involved imagine and enact communities of practice, structuring identities around which prominent acolytes build the walls, denying the fragility of those identities and denying their contingency. An ultimately individualized endeavor, "disciplining" serves primarily to manage dissent and to maintain those raised borders rather than fostering consensus and coalitions (Clifford 2005, 24). There seems always to be someone who argues that borders are necessary. At least some: the positive ones, perhaps. As a compromise, they say. Didn't early anthropology have to distinguish itself from other ethnographic representations that threatened to "overrun" disciplinary boundaries — the travelogues, the missionary reports, the armchair reflections, and the narratives produced by colonial bureaucracies? (Gupta and Ferguson 1998, 29). Doesn't contemporary anthropology still have to do the same or similar?

The only way to find new directions is to reimagine boundaries (Trouillot 2003). To reject borders and their ultimately chaotic persistence exerted through presence, absence, ferocity, and futility. To rethink how those lines are imagined, enforced, and overrun. And, in turn, to rethink how such figures give shape to everything they contain and to everything they obscure. The identities and practices that most persist are often inversions of the excluded — more similar, one to the other, than adherents tend to admit. More fragile, too.

The Fragility of What *Is*

The persistence of diagrams is noteworthy not least because it disrupts the standard, assumed linearity of disciplinary change. Certain diagrammatic forms have persisted even while many "isms" have become "wasms" — the change of tense implying an orderly chronology (Nash 2007). But even when it *might* be said that the discipline has made moves toward a more respectful or inclusive consideration of voices, this typically follows a drawn-out and unacknowledged process of overlooking, mis-hearing, or ignoring those whose work anticipated and long called for such moves, among them people taking feminist or anticolonialist praxis seriously (Nash 2007). For any individual or collective, exploring alternative futures also means starting from where we're at, working with what we have to hand. This means recognizing the contributions of those already working toward similar goals, through shared concerns. It also means resisting any claims of novelty or first-ness, and rejecting overbearing images and ideas that persist in unwelcome, uncritical fashion, and which block the desired moves of solidarity to look beyond, to look elsewhere.

Even resistance has monumentalizing effects. At least, until the monuments are gone. Replaced with a joyful space of absence — a space to gather diverse projected memories and perspectives. Spatial remains. Who wouldn't want to share that space and keep it open for limitless possibilities?

Monuments that are displaced or removed, however, are never truly gone. Seeking to "critically revive" anything means grappling with whatever it is you're rooted in, fighting against, entangled with, and seeking to change. In certain narrow, specific cases, the forceful truth of broader observations becomes even more intense: the "past *is* the present"; "without what *was*, nothing *is*"; and "of the infinite dead, the living are but unimportant bits" (Du Bois 2007, 50, emphasis in original). Those bits are now tasked with building all of our shared futures.

This is the inescapable complicity of turning what *is* and what *was* into what *will be* remembered. How we narrativize a disciplinary history reflects not only which actions are celebrated or forgotten but also who is deemed most responsible for elevating or silencing those diverse acts. The idealization of certain activities is a form of expressing value: common projects taking on their constructed identity through the stories that are repeated and the ideas that are reinforced (Lambek 2010). The process is circular: acts or achievements that are elevated are those that are "narrativizable" — done in order to be recognized and remembered (Graeber 2007). Breaking that circularity involves rejecting the idea that the history of anthropological thought is a "teleological parade of 'isms'" (Singh and Guyer 2016, 197). There is bickering and there are temporary resolutions; but the path is not a linear upward trajectory of careful refinement and development. Perhaps that is why the draw of teleology remains strong: the purpose and value of critique, revealed amid the confusion! Even though, in hindsight, a final cause and formal cause are not always so inseparable. The company we keep and the stories we tell ourselves — dominant ideas of practice — are also shaped as much by the questions that are asked as by the questions that are ignored.

Transgressive Diagrams

The politics of "canon setting" has been driven by trends that reproduce "ando- and Euro-centric biases" and which peripheralize or erase contributions made by peoples of color and women (Harrison 1997, 6). These trends both contribute, and commit, to a particular chronological frame, following a discernible and routinized time line. There remains an "almost instinctive insistence" on replicating the anthropological canon through a narrative arc from the "so-called firsts and founders" to the contested present (Durrani 2019, n.p.). Scholarly timelines delimit whose voices are heard and in what contexts. The assumed linearity of the chronological canon fails to recognize and relay "dispersed histories" that live beyond established routines and confines (Jegathesan 2021). De-linearizing views on time and temporality matters greatly for the task of re-assessing what anthropology — or what any scholarly discipline — is, has been, and what it could or should be doing henceforth.

Understandings of time affect how any interventions are made in the ongoing (re)formulation of disciplinary histories, present purposes, and potential futures. Discussing the politics of time in movements for social change, Sian Lazar (2014) draws on work that distinguishes between *chronos* (mundane time) and *kairos* (momentous time). Any point in time has a *kairos* — a moment of unique potential, a critical opportunity for action — along the continuum of *chronos,* which is quantitative, durational, and measurable time (Miller 1992). The *kairos* has to be grasped in order to generate change, by rupturing the "monotony and repetitiveness" of ceaseless, chronological time (Hardt and Negri 2009, 165). In this view, we can see hindsight as a "co-creation of the past" and the building of collective futures as based on the "co-construction of a narrative" (Lazar 2014, 102–3). Co-creating new narratives and futures means co-creating, or seizing, those qualitatively distinct *kairos* moments. Building in time more than in space. Constructing moments not monuments. The monumentalizing choices that lie behind canon setting have real effects.

The first effect is that scholarly timelines reinforce prejudicial claims about order and interconnection:

> Time lines ensure that events, objects, and people are in their "right place" — temporally, spatially, and politically — so that scholars or laymen can confidently measure changes along time, evaluate novelties, judge directions of influence, assert originality, determine and devalue derivatives, differentiate the unprecedented from precedents, and proclaim turns and turning points. (Azoulay 2019, 168)

Contesting the timeline of anthropology is not to deny that certain "primitivizing and colonizing frameworks" were much more widely endorsed in early anthropology than they are today; rather, it is to challenge the idea that it is ever possible to "evade or escape from our colonial past" (Durrani 2019, n.p.). Plotting those frameworks in their "right place" — in the past — implies that the passing of time has enabled us as anthropologists to move on. That conviction, however, assumes too neat a divide between a disputed, non-critical *then* and a largely resolved, self-correcting *now*. This is the discipline's problematic discourse of "moral perfectibility" that Jobson (2020) calls out.

The second effect is linked to the first: anthropological knowledge production is commonly imagined as being sequential — based on *chronos* — rather than a practice that is immersed in and alert to the critical issues of any particular moment — knowledge generation based on *kairos* (Durrani 2019). The sequential mindset is so pervasive that its dominance goes largely unnoticed, but it limits how knowledge production relates to action. An idea dominates: the idea of gradual refinement, incremental change. Considered reform. A trajectory of steady improvement. No immediacy.

Kairos, by contrast, doesn't want to wait. It involves seeing what needs to be done and orienting actions and outlooks, presently, to address those needs. It is about acting now to dismantle its targets. Of course, these temporal poles actually lie on a spectrum, and the contrasts drawn here are primarily illustrative, not prescriptive. But we recognize a *chronos*-driven account by the way it selectively or artificially isolates present work from prior work, minimizing past crimes and adhering to narratives of incrementality — toward what is imagined to be an always improved and improving realm.

Course correction: a favored mode of reflexivity.

Starting now, what should be done?

But history doesn't start presently.

There is the lopsided inheritance of models and outlooks to figure out.

There are precedents to recognize, to reckon with, to reject, to reformulate.

Of course, we want a brighter future. That is, if we — all of us — are to have a future.

Another reorientation. A refocusing.

Better to choose to see in acts of reappraising anthropological discourse not only the question, "What can anthropologists do?" but also "What have anthropologists already done?" (Rosa and Bonilla 2017, 203). Not only, Where are we now? but also:

How did we get here?

The inverse museum partially reflects that crooked path.

It also acts as an invitation to reimagine how diverse diagrammatic forms, reoriented in these ways, might operate. How could visual metaphors become newly attentive to the construction of relational experience?

What if diagrams were seeking dynamism instead of stasis? What if they were exploring models of thought and pathways-through-imagination that stem from a world in constant movement, amid chaos? If they were embracing *kairos?* Lines that intersect to suggest a rhizomatic "antigenealogy" or other visions for "progeneration" amid an always-changing "relational manifold" (Deleuze and Guattari 1987; Ingold 2000)? How best to undermine just how established diagrams have — almost surreptitiously — become?

> It is also about transforming the image, creating alternatives, asking ourselves questions about what types of images subvert, pose critical alternatives, transform our worldviews and move us away from dualistic thinking about good and bad. Making a space for the transgressive image. (hooks 1992, 4)

This collection does not pretend to catalogue the entire diverse world of diagrams in anthropology. Instead, this collection represents an aesthetic range from across the anthropological corpus — a range that can be read as a snapshot of the discipline's own archive. That institutional archive traces discursive formations that serve multiple purposes in diverse contexts. The diagrams it contains can never escape their moments of origin, creation, and consumption. An archive is never mere memory or document. Rather, the archive comes into being when its handlers wish to mark, repeat, or supplement the origins (or, alternatively, the breakdown) of moments of remembering: without these *outside* acts, there is no archive (Derrida 1995). This collection invites renewed engagements with what have become monumental works, ideas, and practices — engagements that themselves constitute outside acts and reflections.

This collection invites a reappraisal also of how we can read diagrams in anthropology — historically, critically, and creatively. In the present, each reading of a diagram — each time someone engages with a diagram and makes interpretations of its contents — is an act that positions the reader within overlapping cognitive and historical processes. Those seriated processes remain incomplete. The dissimilarity of diagrams makes demands of each new reader who responds in relation to their own context and concerns (Bender and Marrinan 2010, 8). What would it mean to read "without guarantee" (Hall 1986)? A process of reading in which "its terms, affordances, and stakes cannot be declared and secured beforehand" (Brinkema 2022, 21)? To create a space of radical openness: an orientation that is implicated in defining and rejecting its own ethical and epistemological limitations.

Diagrammatic forms require a reader to interpret multiple scales, foci, and resolutions, and to actively correlate information spread across those diverse forms (Bender and Marrinan 2010, 8). The act of reading is not only interpretative, it is also selective, critical, and relational. Committing to that relationality — as both a methodological and ethical basis for engaging in knowledge (co)creation — means recognizing how shared histories and the different ways in which different people are implicated in them constitute the ground for critical practice. This is a double-movement that identifies the shared ideas and referents in common that facilitate expression and communication while also questioning the necessity of particular forms for achieving shared goals, expanding the range of those goals in the process.

How have shifts in approaches to knowledge, evidence, and representation changed diagrams and their roles in contemporary anthropological practice? Briefly, again, allowing an expansive "we" to include anyone who uses the word "anthropology" to describe their work or those whose work is recognized with the same term by an active community of scholars or collaborators: What are the criteria we use to assess and understand diagrams, what are our expectations of them, and how do they relate to processes of knowledge-creation more broadly? What approaches to *the diagram* more broadly could open spaces of reappraisal for these visual anthropological works?

Part II of this book, "Images Gathered (A Fragmented Crowd)," contains a collection of 52 diagrams: the basis of this Inverse Museum. Together, these images invite further reflection on the possibilities that diagrams variously suggest or enable, grounding the discussion that follows. Eighteen diagrams are selected and subsequently examined in more detail. Part III, "Inversions, Continued," studies the contested relationships between visual devices and other related modes of ethnographic exploration with anthropology's disciplinary norms, frameworks, fixations, and models. Part IV, "Excess (Possibilities)," extends the discussion of diagrams through their connection to anthropology's core methodological and political issues of temporality, relationality, potentiality, and positionality. Part V, "Burning to Prepare The Ground," concludes with a discussion of how inverse or reworked histories of (diagrams in) anthropology can support revived forms of visual, political, and relational praxis.

II

Images Gathered
(A Fragmented Crowd)

Bibliographic information and analysis for all 52 images is provided in Part VI, "Sources."

This collection spans 150 years. Commonalities are few. Many are presented in this section without context — the focus is on their aesthetics. Without explanation, they appear inscrutable. But they are all evocative. They each hint at potentialities. Elsewhere, there are many more, and more impenetrable, diagrams to be found, especially in the fields of biological anthropology, linguistic anthropology, and archaeology. Typically, though, such examples are explicit in their scientistic orientation, with those from the biological anthropology more troubling still in their reductive, violent quantification of others and their imposition of researcher-defined categories of social difference. The images selected here instead draw on sociocultural anthropology while also speaking to and drawing influence from diagrammatic approaches, interests, and practices from across a number of other fields — including philosophy, postcolonial studies, collaborative community-based research, and critical art theory.

The images vary widely in style, design, approach, and content. Almost any arrangement of lines drawn to illustrate some aspect, dynamic, measurement, or reflection of either social life or conceptual thought can be, and often has been, considered a diagram. This range reflects the creativity poured into visualizations of different kinds, expanding way beyond the familiar kinship diagram — which is perhaps *the* classical visual referent within anthropology. For decades, it practically became a disciplinary requirement for the work of "every ethnographer" to include an illustrated description of the relevant "kinship system" (Barnard and Good 1984, 1). As Mary Bouquet points out, this meant presenting genealogical charts and kinship diagrams, which became omnipresent and which still feature widely across anthropological publications — making it all the more conspicuous that the theoretical status of these constructions has rarely been considered (Bouquet 1996, 43). Just as disciplinary debates and demands have changed — kinship is one of many concepts variously contested, defended, and critiqued as an "artifact of the anthropologist's analytical apparatus" (Schneider 1984, vii), or revived in more relational terms (e.g. Carsten 2004) — so have critical accounts of the political and ethical implications of writing about and visualizing the lives of others. These images invite further reflection on broad, exploratory questions concerning anthropological purposes, possibilities, and politics.

This collection of images can be read independently of the discussion sections that follow. I have made curatorial choices not to represent or reinforce a canon but instead to contribute to the unfinished work of exploring persistences and potentialities across diverse diagrammatic forms.

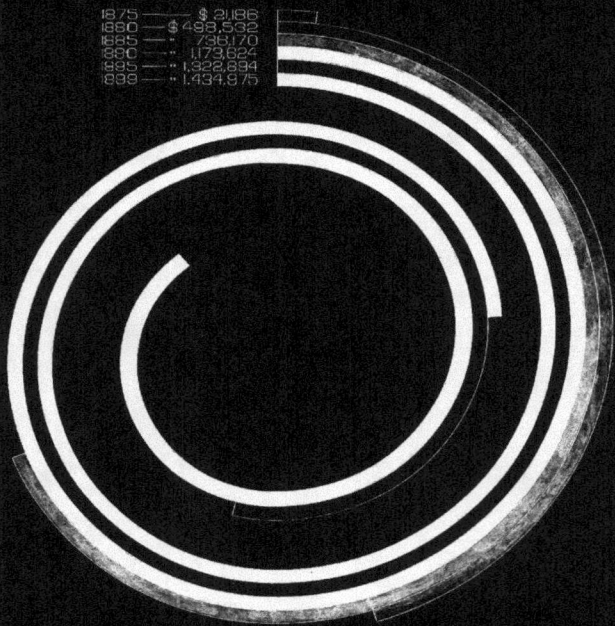

1875 —— $ 21,186
1880 —— $ 498,532
1885 —— " 736,170
1890 —— " 1,173,624
1895 —— " 1,322,894
1899 —— " 1,434,975

(Du Bois 1900, d1)

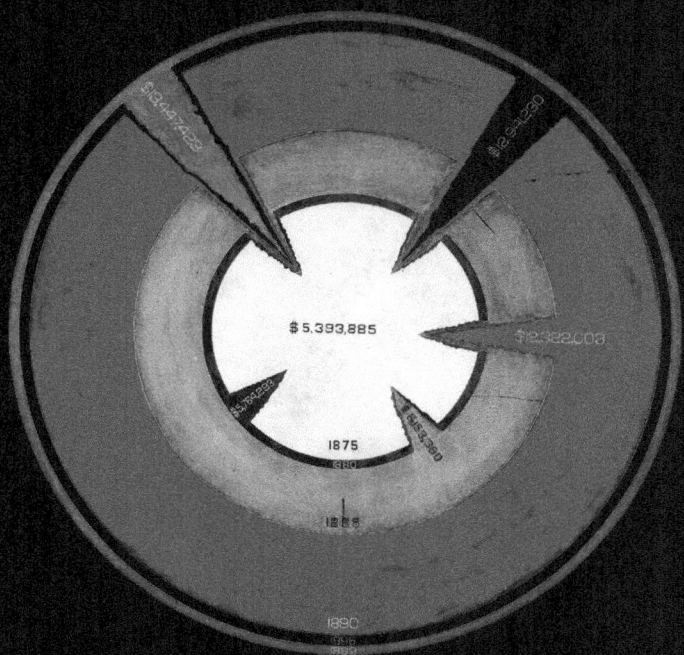

$ 5.393,885

$13,447,459

$194,290

$12,382,003

$5,780,293

$1,853,290

1875

1880

1885

1890

(Du Bois 1900, d2)

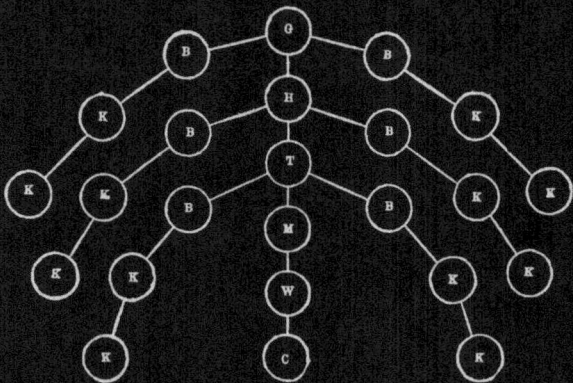

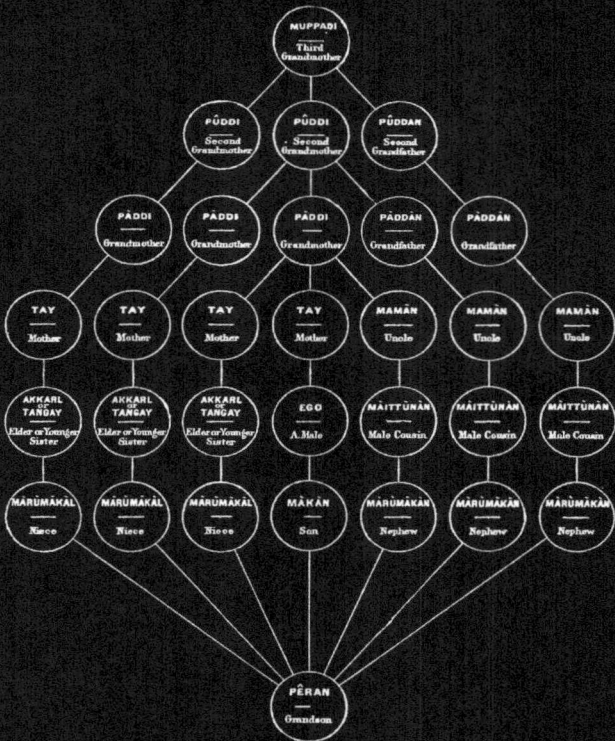

(Morgan 1871, 46, 595)

(Morgan 1871, 605)

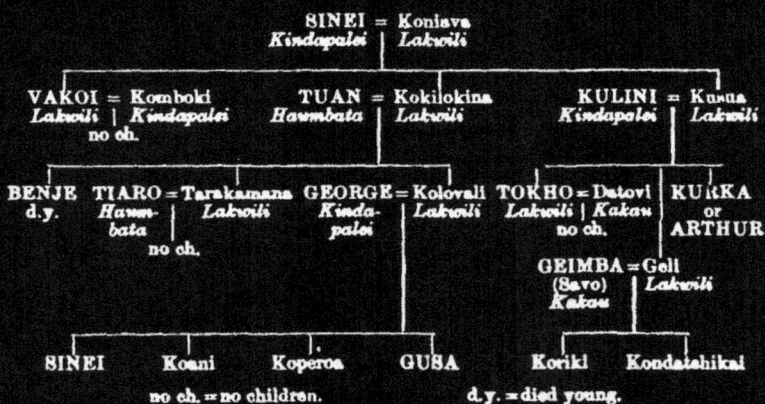

SINEI = Koniava
Kindapalei | *Lakwili*

VAKOI = Komboki   TUAN = Kokilokina   KULINI = Kunua
Lakwili | *Kindapalei* *Hawmbata* | *Lakwili*   *Kindapalei* | *Lakwili*
no ch.

BENJE TIARO = Tarakamana   GEORGE = Kolovali   TOKHO = Datovi   KUitKA
d.y.   *Hawm-* | *Lakwili*   *Kinda-* | *Lakwili* *Lakwili* | *Kakau*   or
       bata   *palei*   no ch.   ARTHUR
       no ch.

                                                  GEIMBA = Gell
                                                  (Savo) | *Lakwili*
                                                  Kakau

SINEI   Koani   Koperoa   GUSA   Korikl   Kondatshikai
       no ch. = no children.   d.y. = died young.

(Rivers 1910, 1)

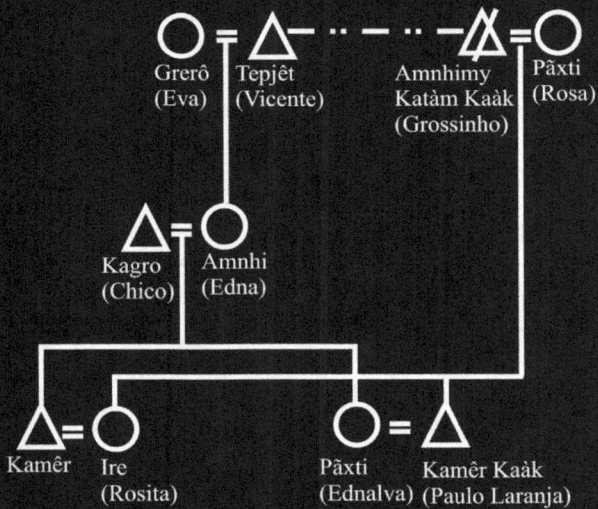

Grerô   Tepjêt   Amnhimy   Pãxti
(Eva)   (Vicente)   Katàm Kaàk   (Rosa)
                                   (Grossinho)

Kagro   Amnhi
(Chico) (Edna)

Kamêr   Ire   Pãxti   Kamêr Kaàk
        (Rosita)   (Ednalva)   (Paulo Laranja)

(Giraldin 2011, 421)

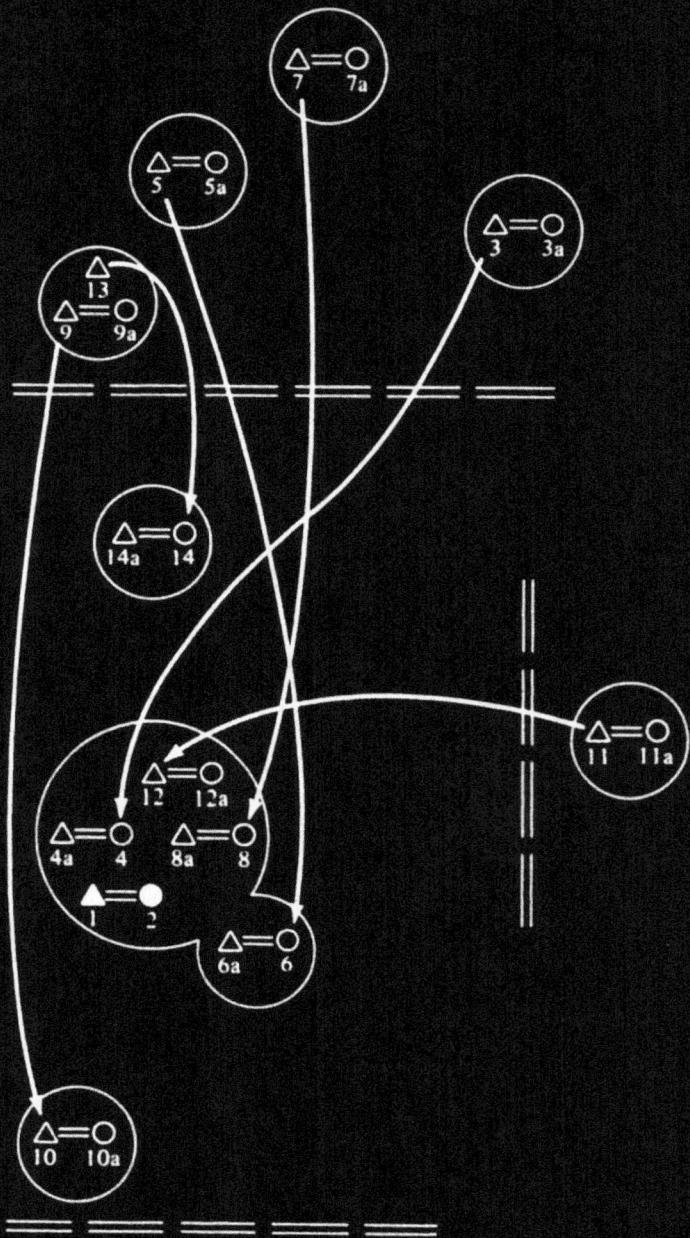

(Munn 1986, 1)

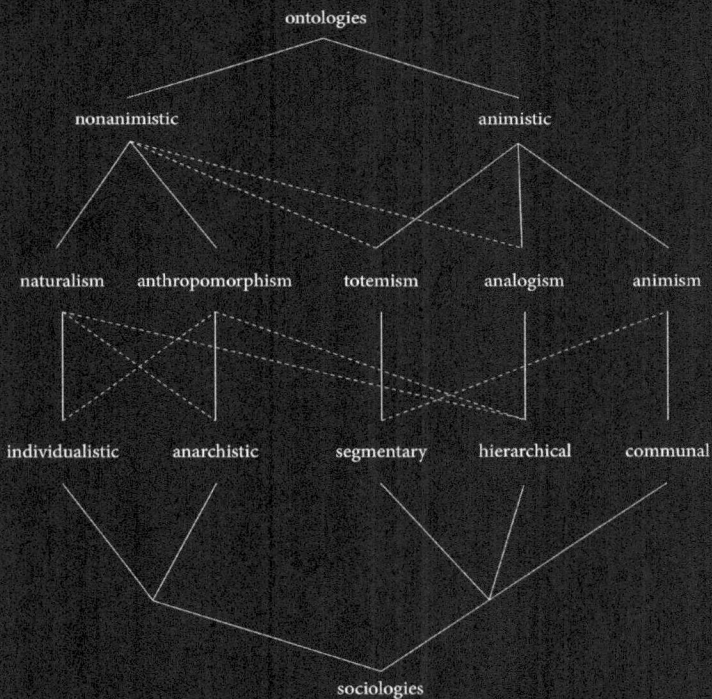

ontologies

nonanimistic   animistic

naturalism   anthropomorphism   totemism   analogism   animism

individualistic   anarchistic   segmentary   hierarchical   communal

sociologies

(de Almeida 2014, 293)

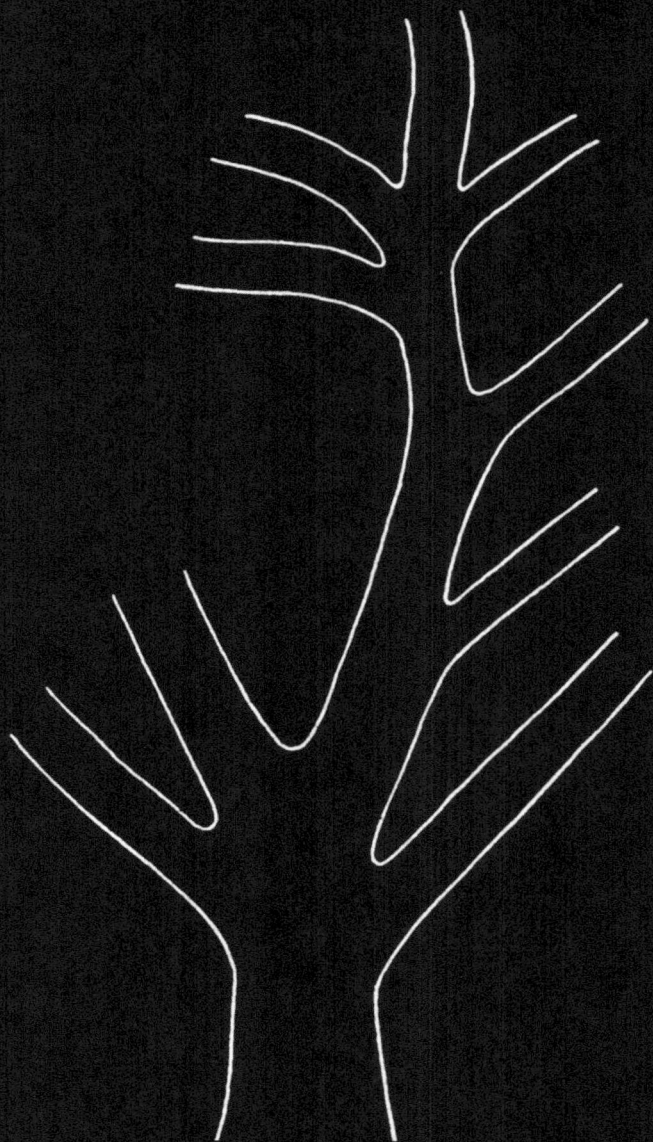

(after Evans-Pritchard 1940, 196–97)

(after Evans-Pritchard 1940, 196–97)

(after Evans-Pritchard 1940, 201–2)

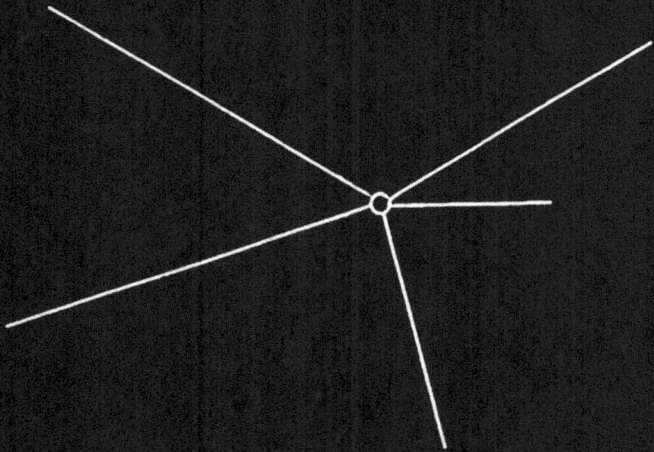

(after Evans-Pritchard 1940, 201–2)

(Herskovits 1952, 296)

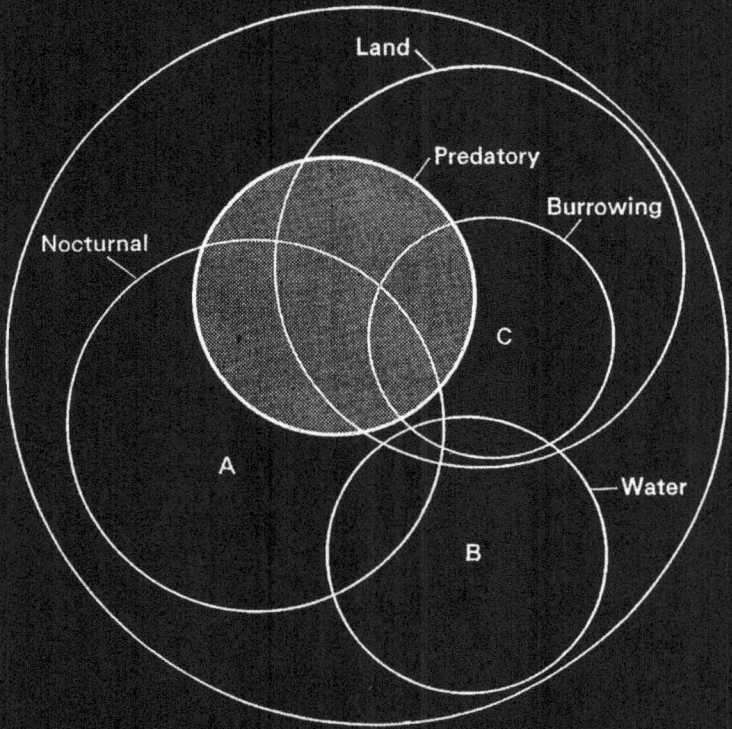

(Douglas 2003, 271)

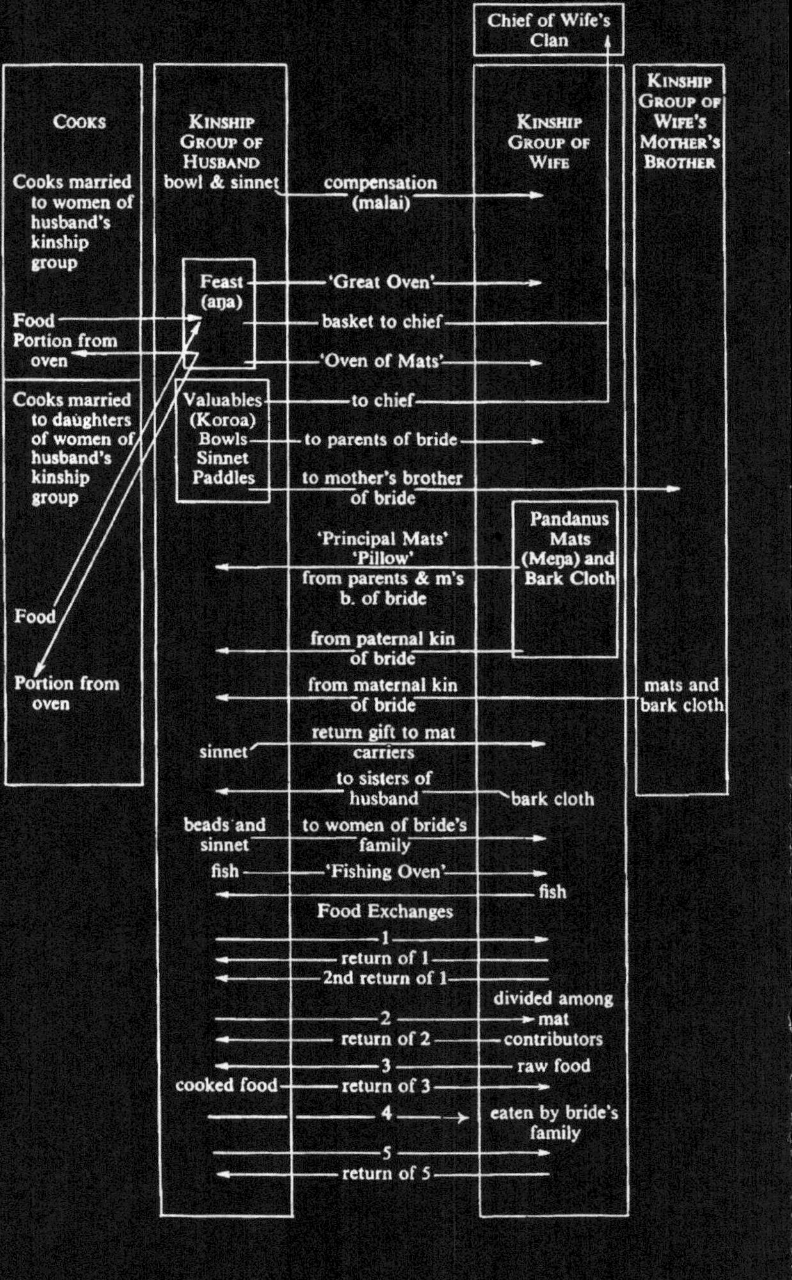

Chief of Wife's Clan

COOKS	KINSHIP GROUP OF HUSBAND	KINSHIP GROUP OF WIFE	KINSHIP GROUP OF WIFE'S MOTHER'S BROTHER

Cooks married to women of husband's kinship group

bowl & sinnet

compensation (malai)

Feast (aṇa)

Food Portion from oven

'Great Oven'

basket to chief

'Oven of Mats'

Cooks married to daughters of women of husband's kinship group

Valuables (Koroa) Bowls Sinnet Paddles

to chief

to parents of bride

to mother's brother of bride

Pandanus Mats (Meṇa) and Bark Cloth

'Principal Mats' 'Pillow' from parents & m's b. of bride

from paternal kin of bride

Food

Portion from oven

from maternal kin of bride

mats and bark cloth

sinnet

return gift to mat carriers

to sisters of husband

bark cloth

beads and sinnet

to women of bride's family

fish

'Fishing Oven'

fish

Food Exchanges

1

return of 1

2nd return of 1

2

divided among mat contributors

return of 2

3

raw food

cooked food

return of 3

4

eaten by bride's family

5

return of 5

(Lévi-Strauss 1969, 64)

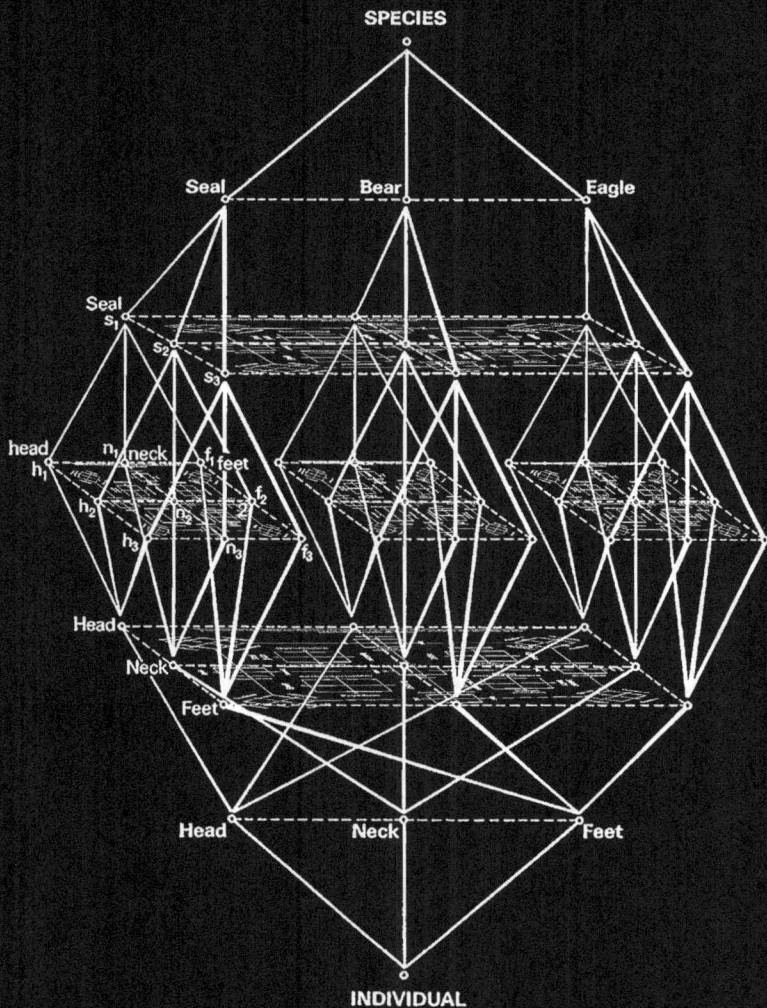

(Lévi-Strauss 1966, 152)

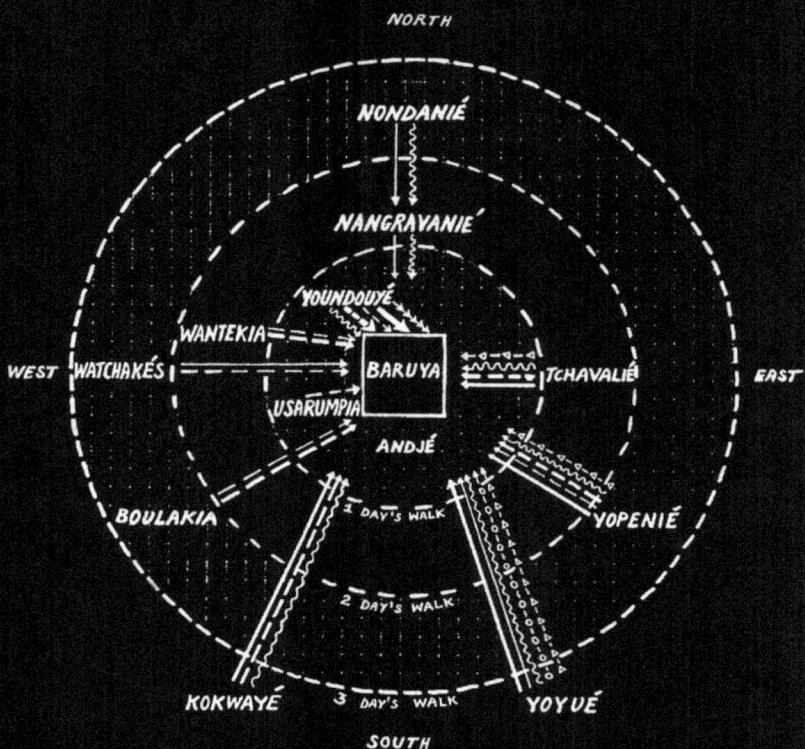

NORTH

NONDANIÉ

NANGRAVANIÉ

YOUNDOUYÉ

WANTEKIA

WEST WATCHAKÉS BARUYA TCHAVALIÉ EAST

USARUMPIA

ANDJÉ

BOULAKIA 1 DAY'S WALK YOPENIÉ

2 DAY'S WALK

KOKWAYÉ 3 DAY'S WALK YOYUÉ

SOUTH

BARUYA TRADING PARTNERS

BOW + BARBED ARROWS →→→	STONE ADZES ———→
FEATHERS — — — →	STEEL AXES ———→
BARKCLOTH – – – →	SHELLS ∿∿∿→
PIGS –o–o–o–o→	DOGS –△–△–△→

(Jablonko & Godelier 1983)

(Conklin 1980, 13)

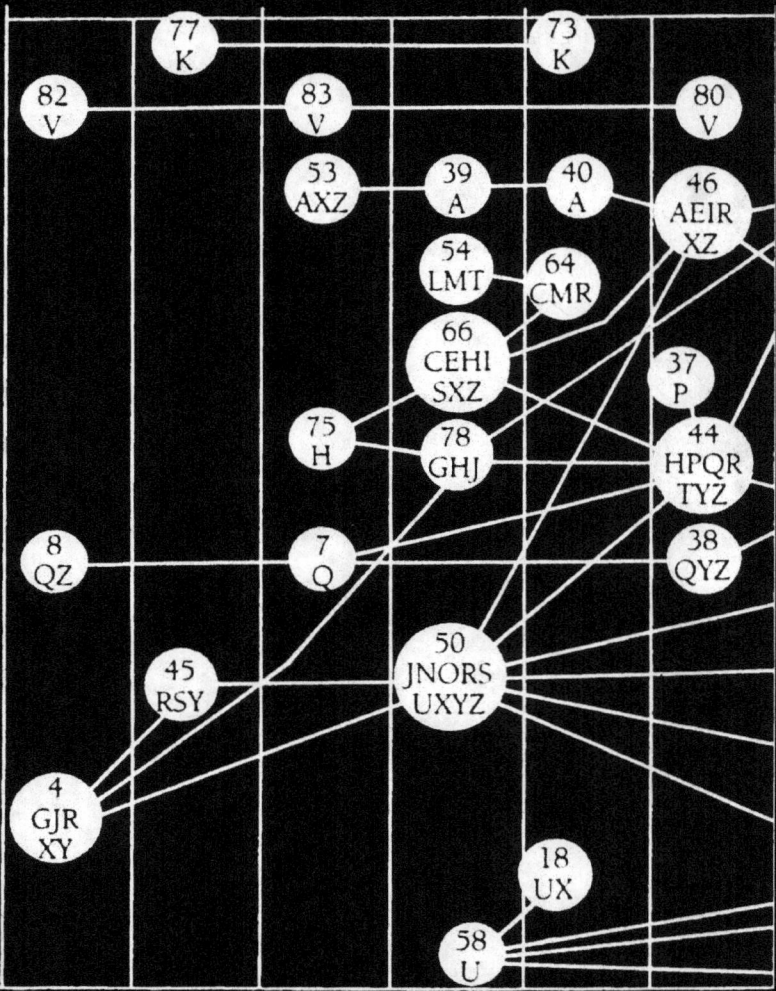

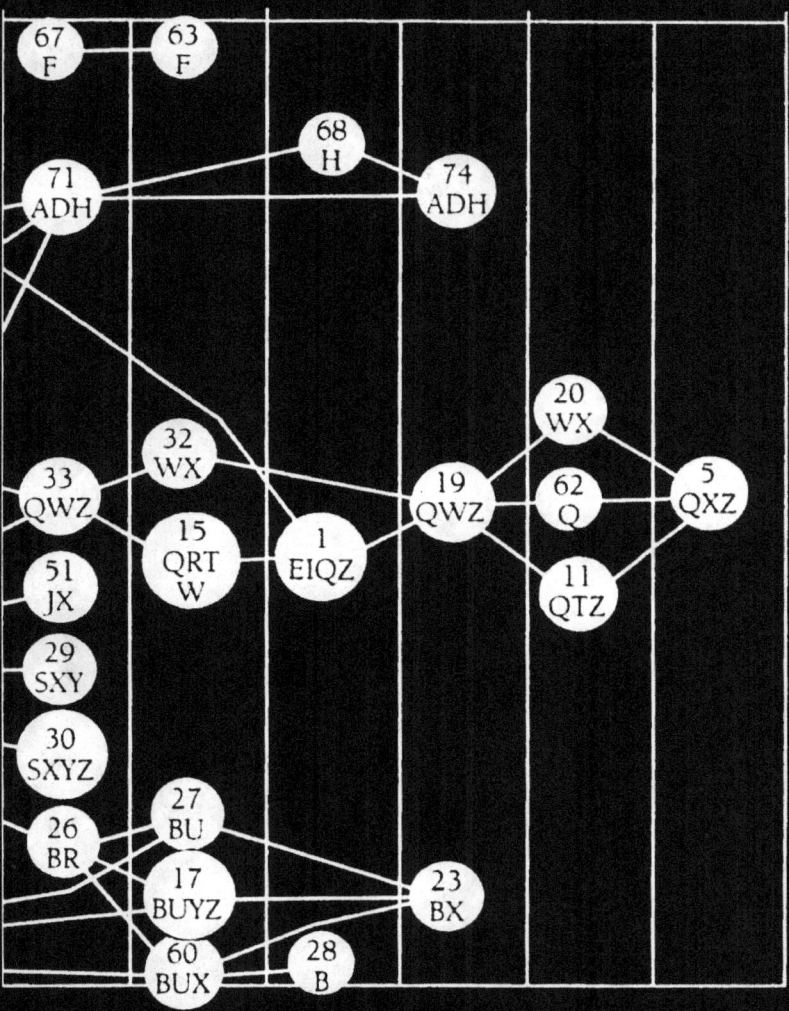

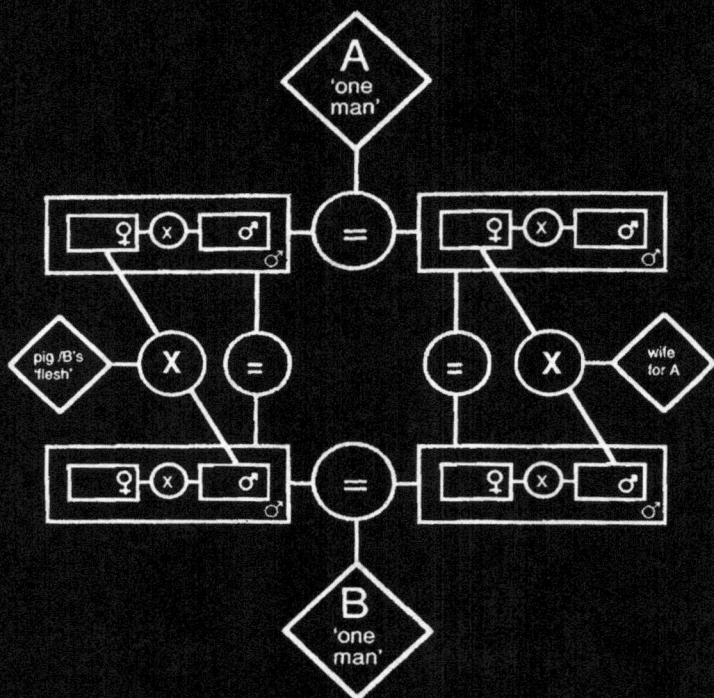

(Gell 1999, 64)

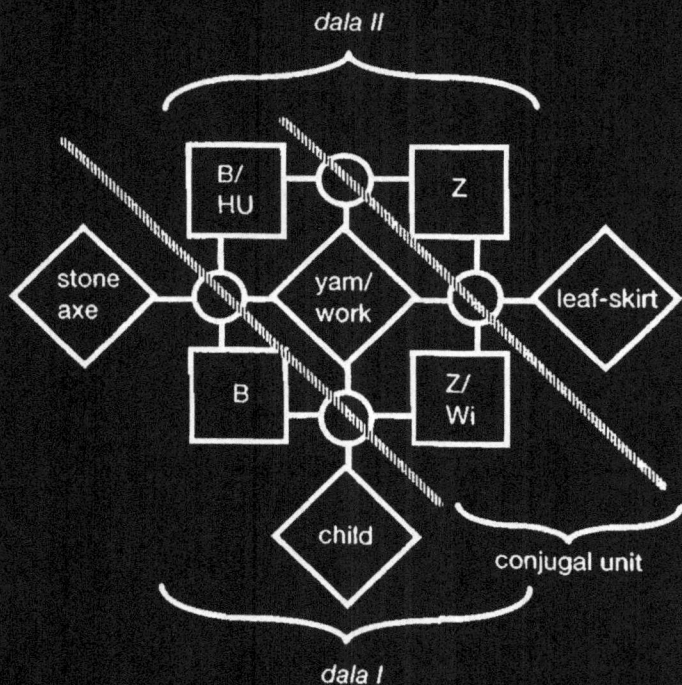

(Gell 1999, 72)

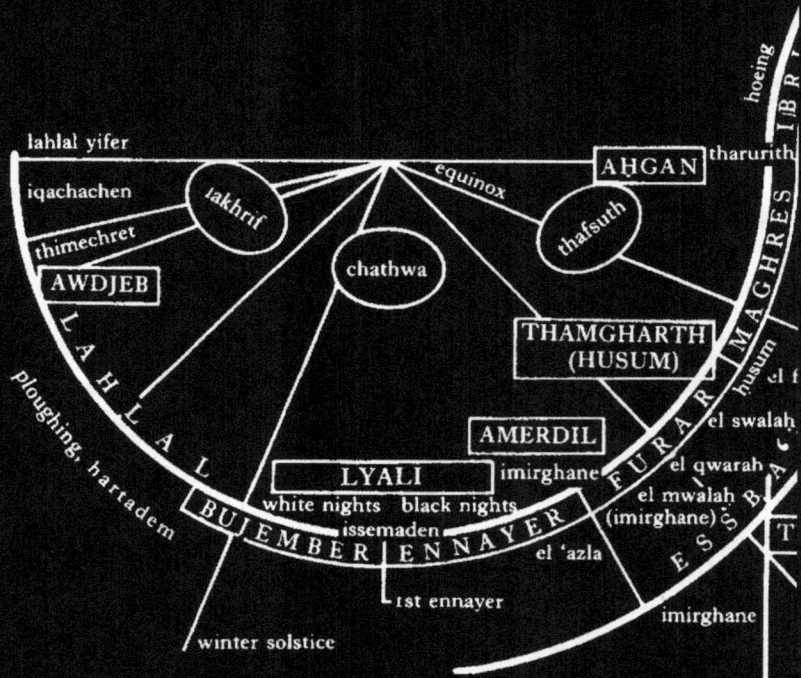

X

mut
1st day of

NISAN

hoeing

tharurith

AHGAN

equinox

lahlal yifer

iqachachen

iakhrif

thafsuth

thimechret

AWDJEB

chathwa

THAMGHARTH
(HUSUM)

el f

el swalah

AMERDIL

el qwarah

ploughing, hartadem

LYALI

imirghane

el mwalah
(imirghane)

white nights   black nights

T

issemaden

BUJEMBER ENNAYER

el 'azla

1st ennayer

imirghane

winter solstice

Y

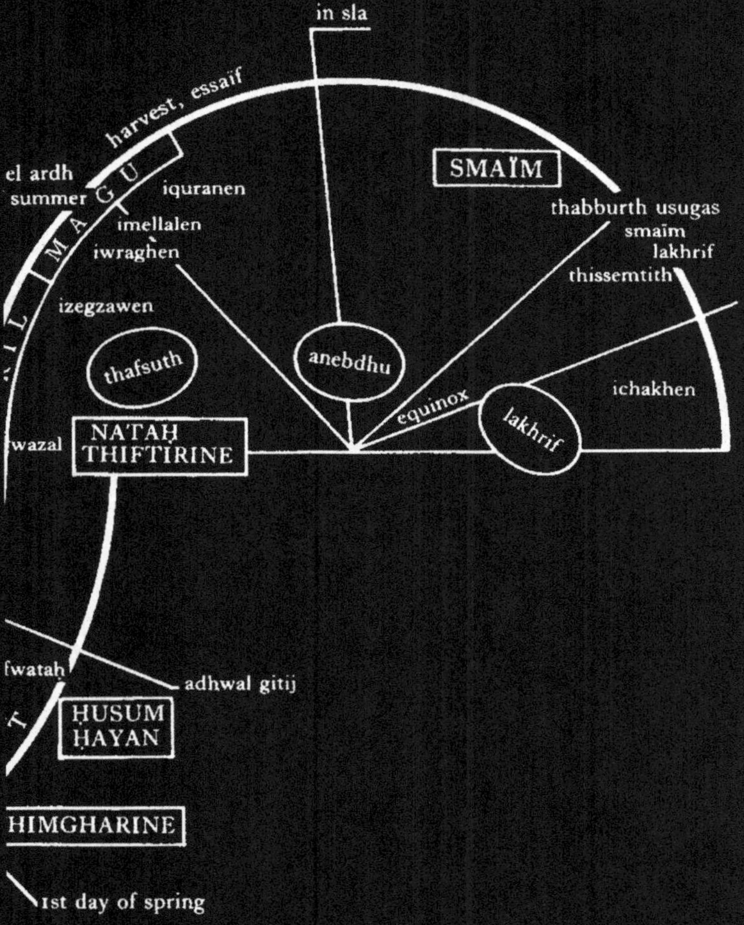

in sla

harvest, essaif

el ardh
summer

SMAÏM

iquranen

thabburth usugas
smaïm
lakhrif
thissemtith

imellalen
iwraghen

izegzawen

thafsuth

anebdhu

ichakhen

lakhrif

equinox

wazal

NATAḤ
THIFTIRINE

fwatah

adhwal gitij

ḤUSUM
ḤAYAN

HIMGHARINE

1st day of spring

(Bourdieu 1977, 99)

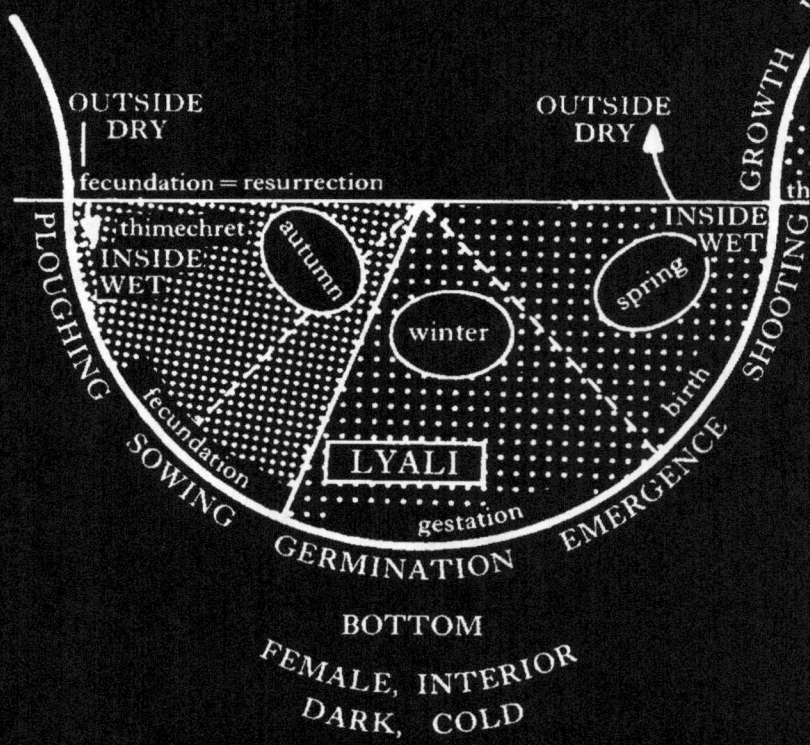

OUTSIDE DRY

OUTSIDE DRY

fecundation = resurrection

PLOUGHING

thimechret

INSIDE WET

autumn

INSIDE WET

spring

GROWTH

th

SHOOTING

winter

fecundation

LYALI

birth

SOWING

gestation

EMERGENCE

GERMINATION

BOTTOM
FEMALE, INTERIOR
DARK, COLD

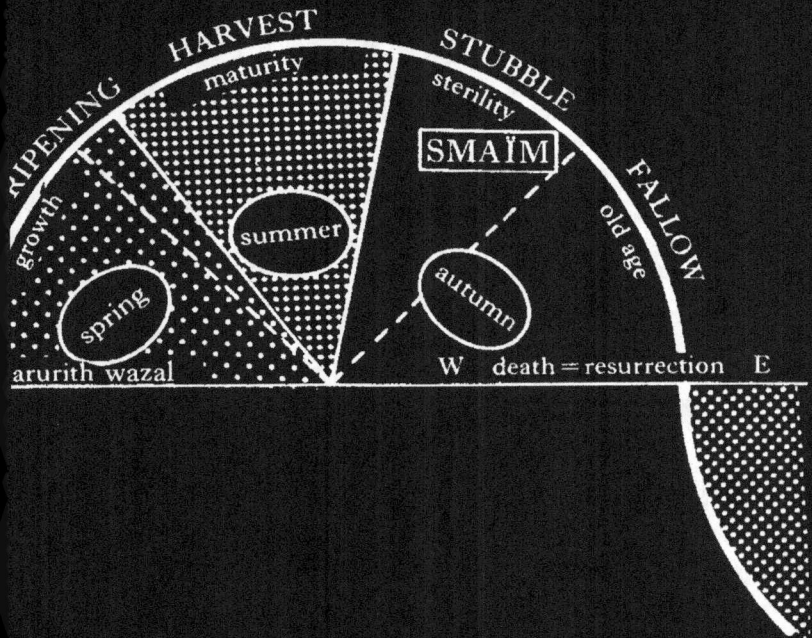

(Bourdieu 1977, 134)

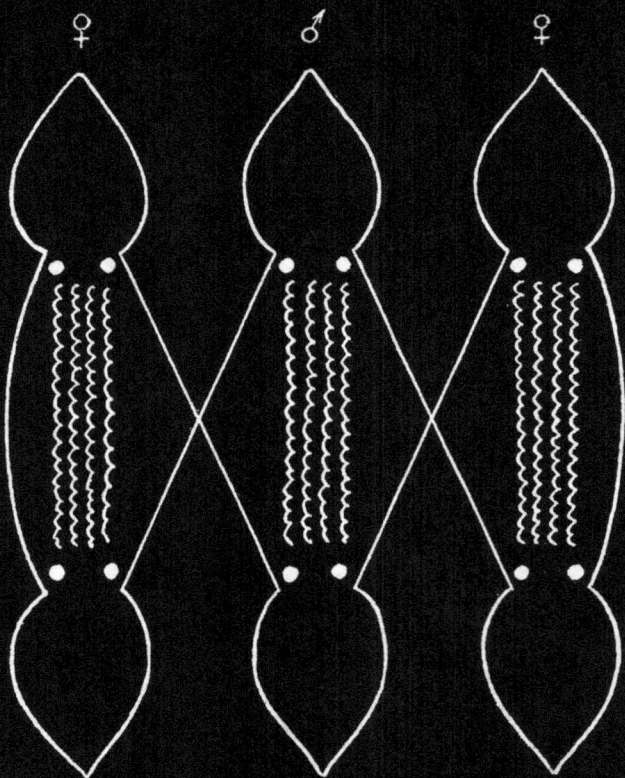

(Deacon & Wedgwood 1934, 163)

(Deacon & Wedgwood 1934, 161)

THE NIVENS FROM
FLORENCE
THE LIFT
THE BATHROOM
THE TARDIS/ LUMBER-ROOM
PARENT'S BEDROOM
BOB'S BEDROOM
DOWNSTAIRS
TIMELINE
1968
1978
1988
RENT
FIGHT

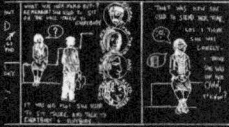

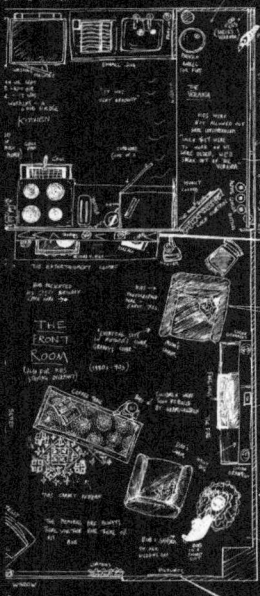
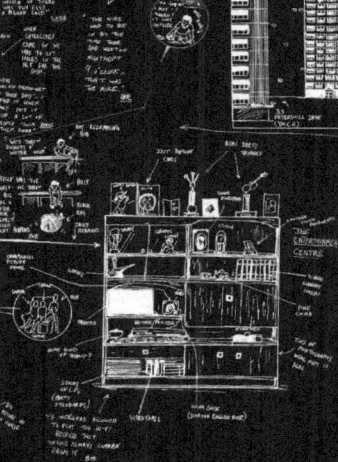

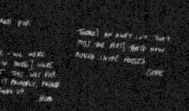

(Miller n.d.)

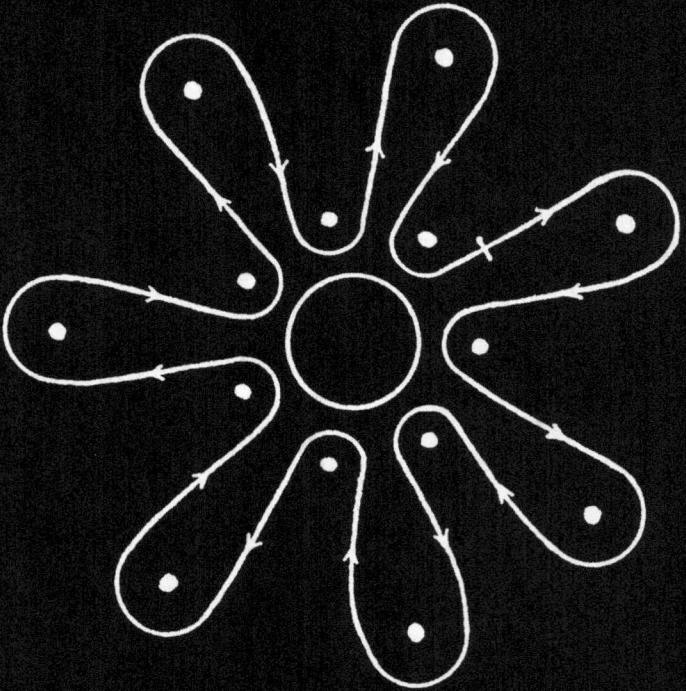

(Deacon & Wedgwood 1934, 170)

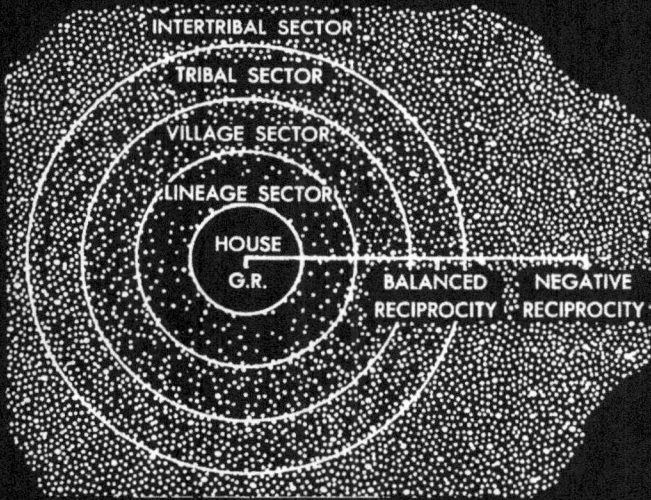

INTERTRIBAL SECTOR
TRIBAL SECTOR
VILLAGE SECTOR
LINEAGE SECTOR
HOUSE
G.R.
BALANCED   NEGATIVE
RECIPROCITY   RECIPROCITY

(Sahlins 1972, 199)

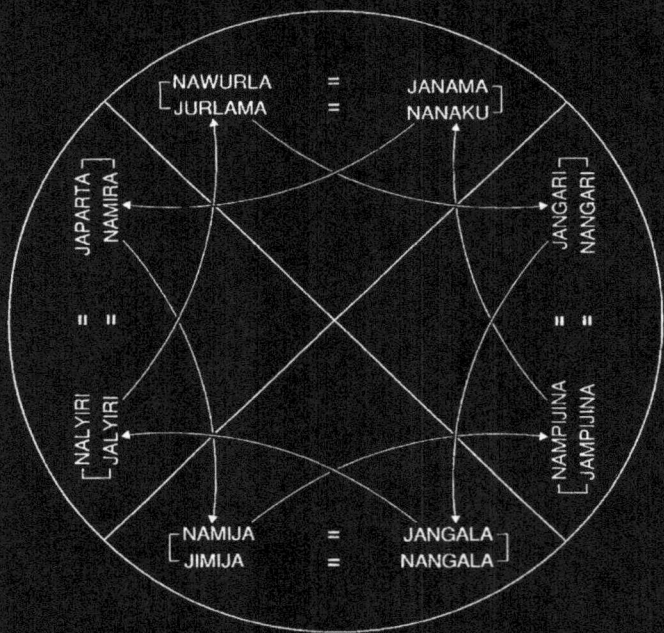

(Rose 2000, 77)

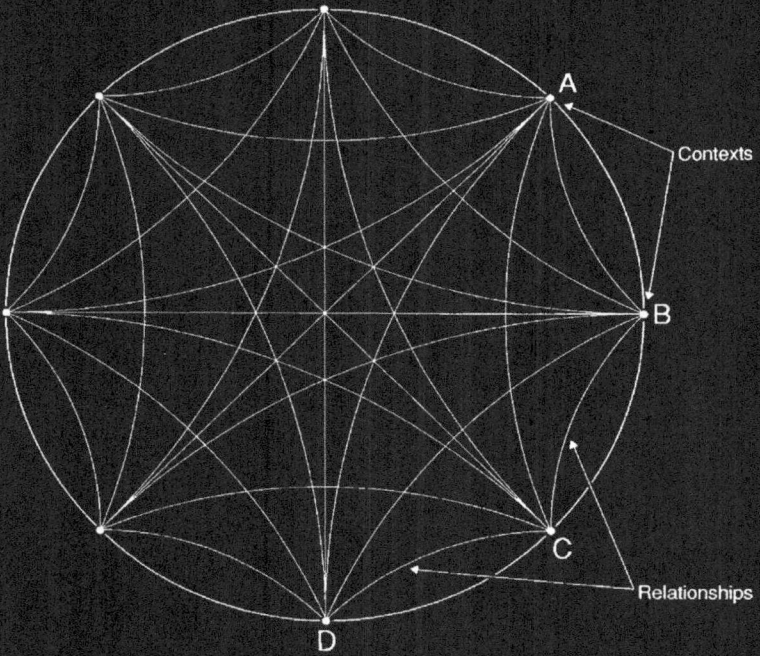

(Rose 2000, 222)

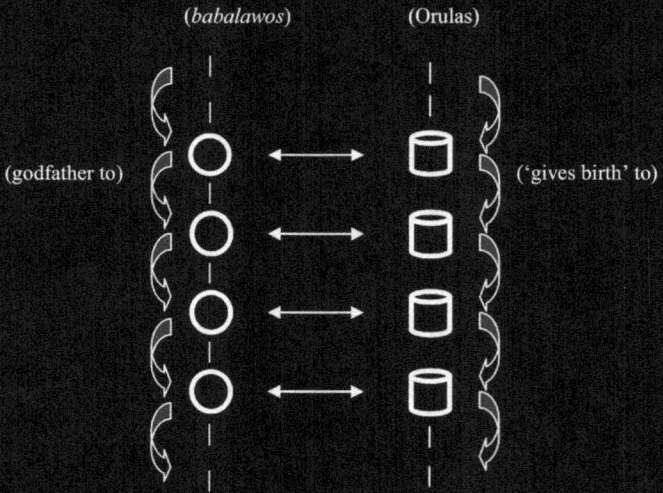

(babalawos)   (Orulas)

(godfather to)   ('gives birth' to)

(Holbraad 2012, 95)

A. Conjunction
(causal links)

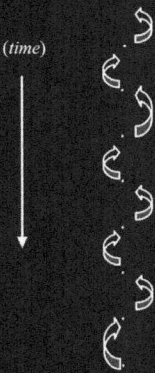

B. Coincidence
(non-causal interactions)

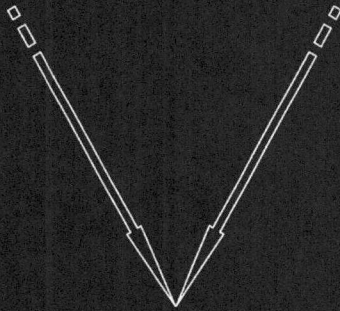

(*time*)

· : *event,* ⪦ : *causal link* (consequent to antecedent), ▭⟹ : *trajectory of motion*

(Holbraad 2012, 199)

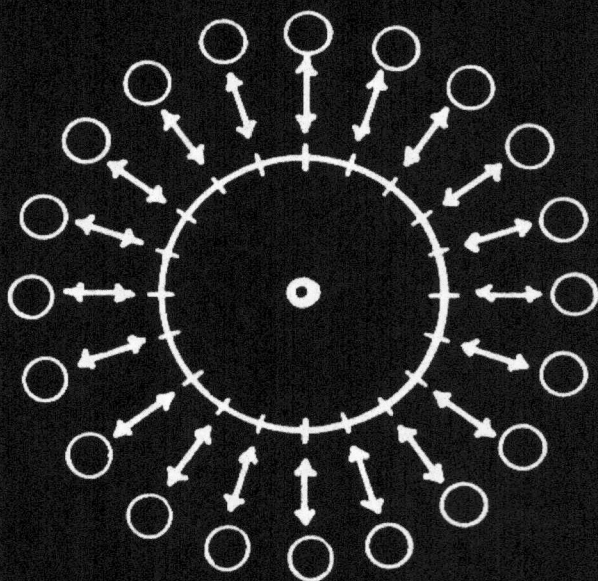

(Mimica 1988, 71)

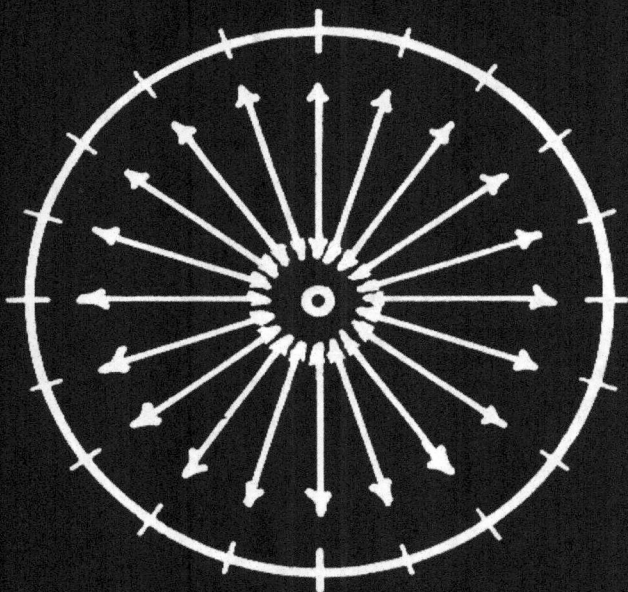

(Mimica 1988, 71)

(Layard 1936, 150)

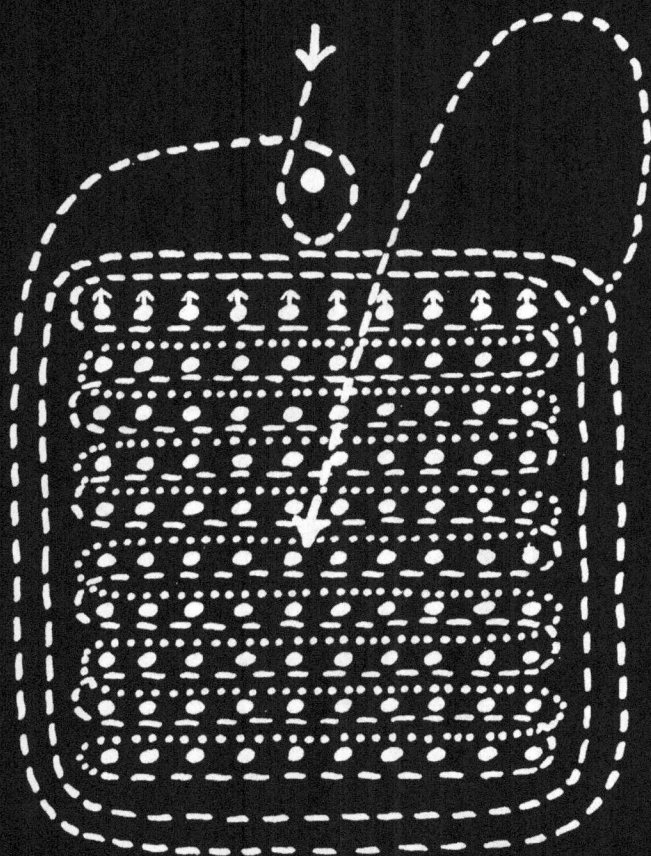

(Layard 1936, 158)

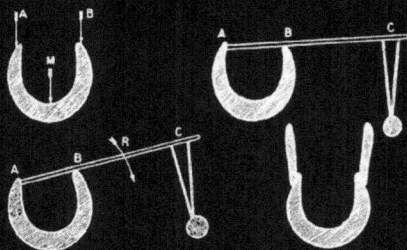

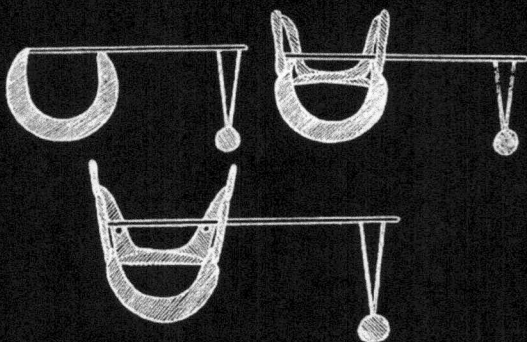

(Malinowski 1922, 109, 111)

(Law & Lien 2018, 148)

TUI NI AO

TIA RUGA A TAHA

NGARUE TE FATU-MOANA

O RAGI TA KE

TIKONU ARIKI

TURI HONO

TETUMU O KUPORU

TURE ORA

PEAHA

RAGI NO
TUMU PO
TUMU HARURU
TAPATAPA I AHA
TE PIU HONUA
MATAU HITI
ONOVARU
KORORUPE
TUARATI

(Young 1919, 210a)

A

B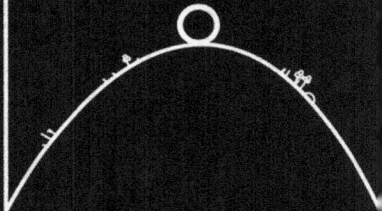

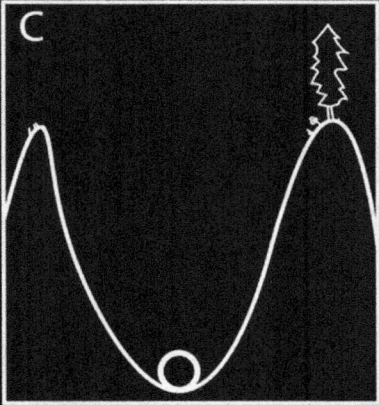

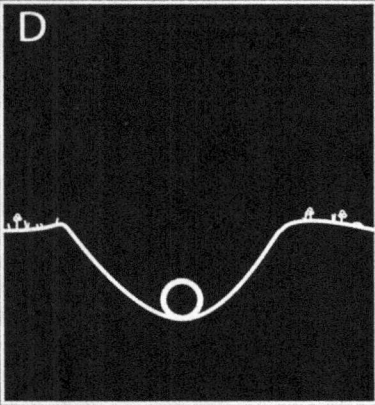

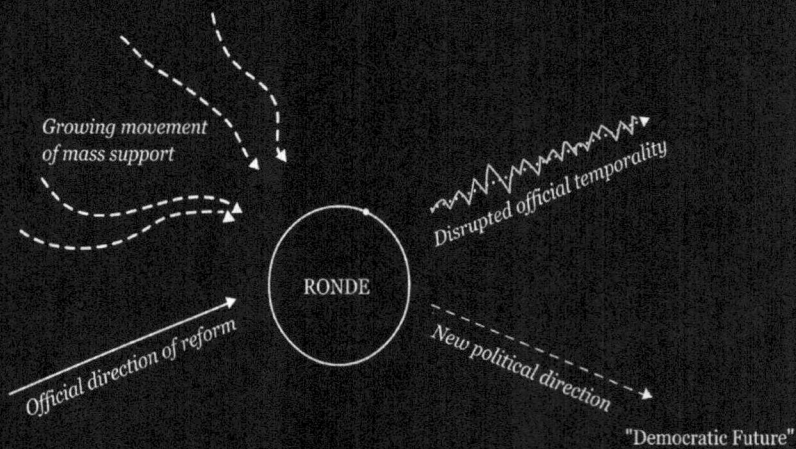

Growing movement
of mass support

Disrupted official temporality

RONDE

Official direction of reform

New political direction

"Democratic Future"

(Thorkelson 2016, 507)

CONSTITUENTS

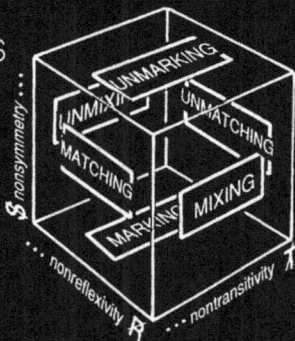

human aims
(puruṣārthas)

release

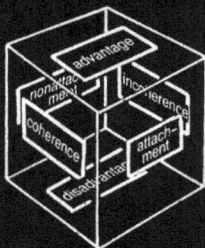

world

elements
(bhutas)

ether

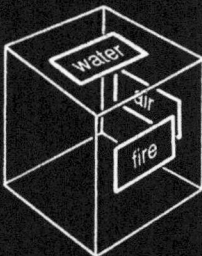

earth

strands
(guṇas)

strandless

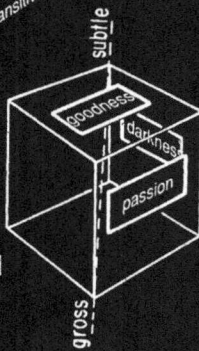

stranded

humors
(doṣas)

spaces

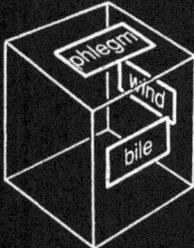

body

(Marriott 1989, 10)

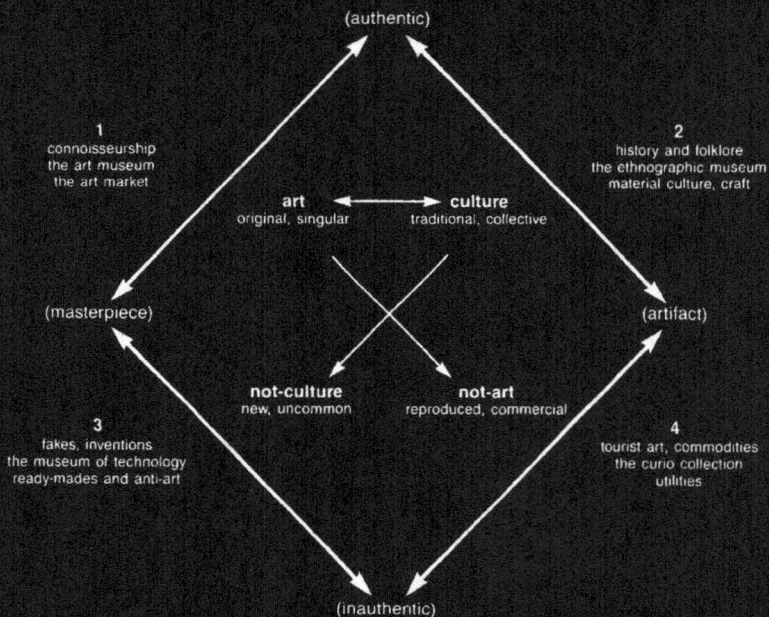

(authentic)

1
connoisseurship
the art museum
the art market

2
history and folklore
the ethnographic museum
material culture, craft

art
original, singular

culture
traditional, collective

(masterpiece)

(artifact)

not-culture
new, uncommon

not-art
reproduced, commercial

3
fakes, inventions
the museum of technology
ready-mades and anti-art

4
tourist art, commodities
the curio collection
utilities

(inauthentic)

(Clifford 1988, 224)

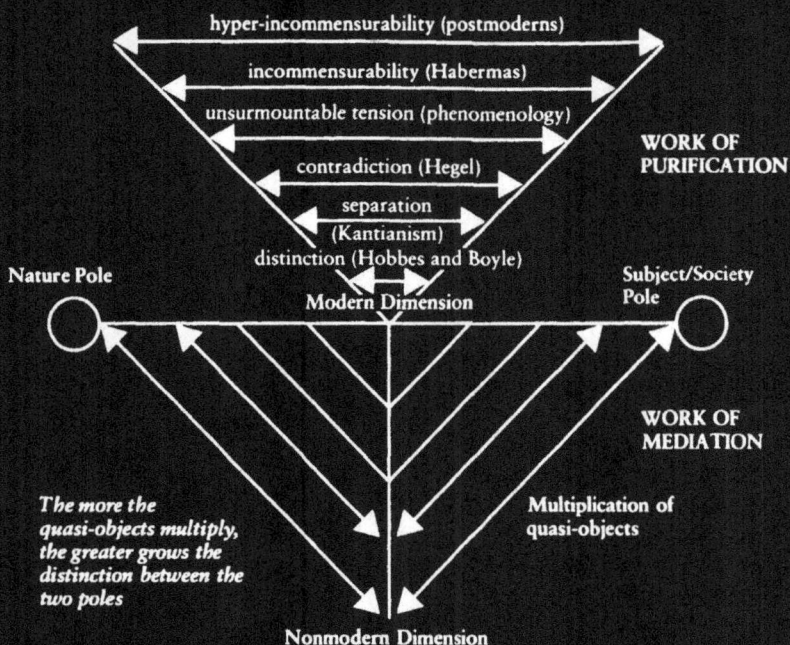

hyper-incommensurability (postmoderns)

incommensurability (Habermas)

unsurmountable tension (phenomenology)

contradiction (Hegel)

separation
(Kantianism)

distinction (Hobbes and Boyle)

WORK OF
PURIFICATION

Nature Pole

Subject/Society
Pole

Modern Dimension

WORK OF
MEDIATION

*The more the
quasi-objects multiply,
the greater grows the
distinction between the
two poles*

Multiplication of
quasi-objects

Nonmodern Dimension

(Latour 1993, 58)

(after Chavez 2012)

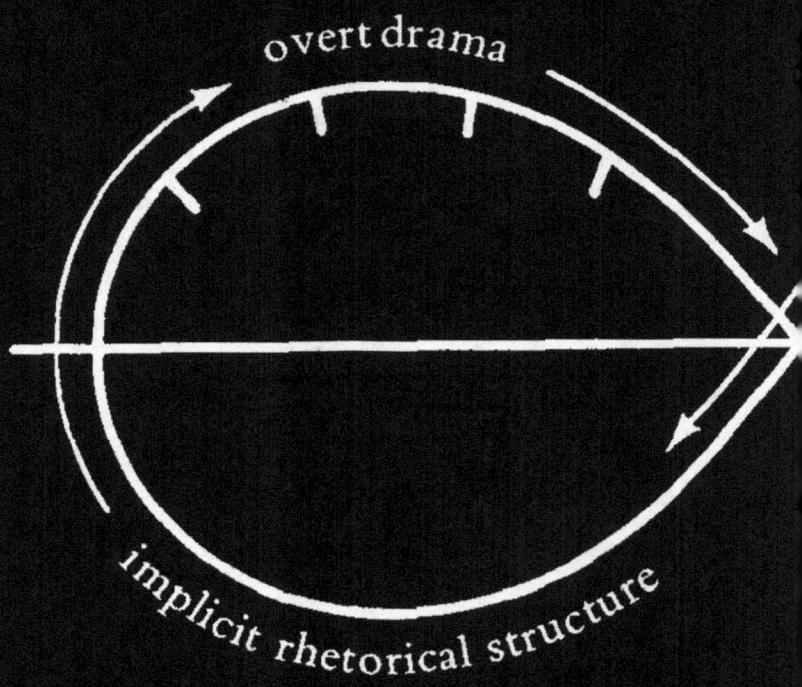

Social Drama

overt drama

implicit rhetorical structure

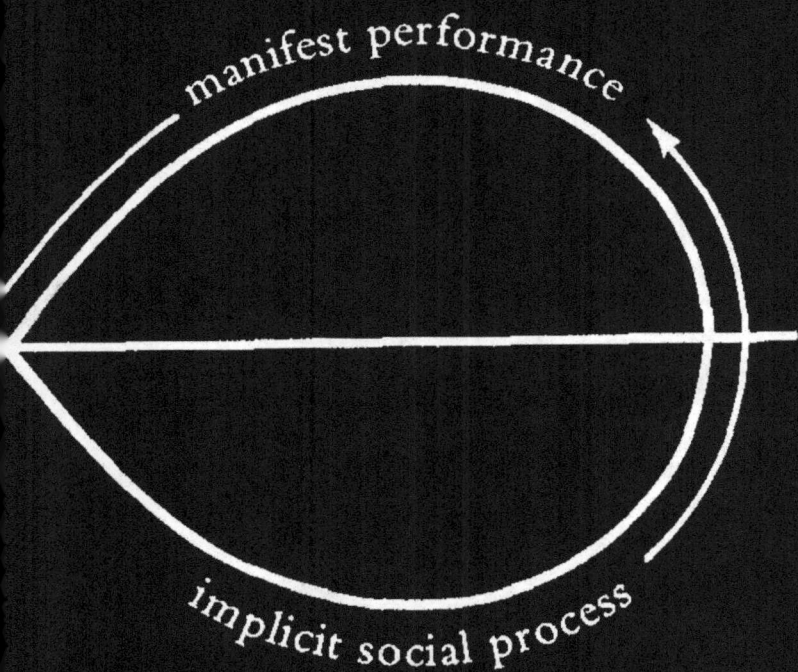

Stage Drama

manifest performance

implicit social process

(Turner 1985, 300)

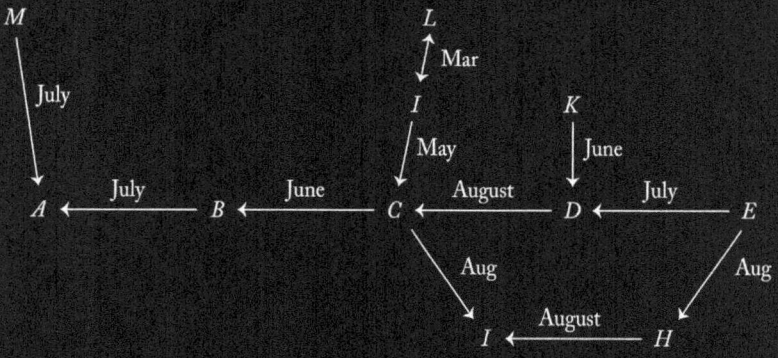

M

July

L

Mar

I

K

May

June

A ← July ← B ← June ← C ← August ← D ← July ← E

Aug

Aug

I ← August ← H

(Gregory 2015, 58)

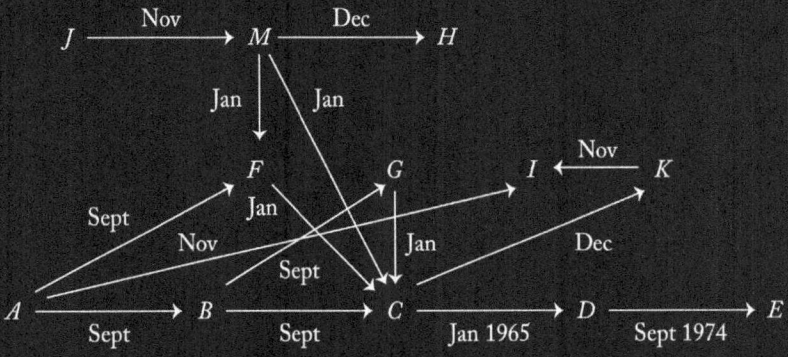

(Gregory 2015, 59)

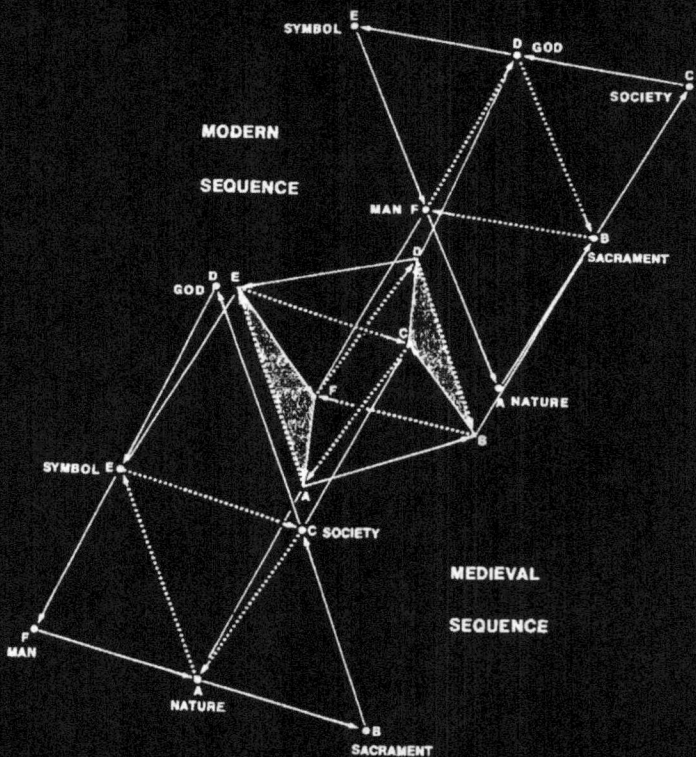

MODERN
SEQUENCE

SYMBOL E

D GOD

C
SOCIETY

MAN F

B
SACRAMENT

GOD D E

D

C

F

A NATURE

B

SYMBOL E

C SOCIETY

MEDIEVAL
SEQUENCE

F
MAN

A
NATURE

B
SACRAMENT

(Gregory 2015, 59)

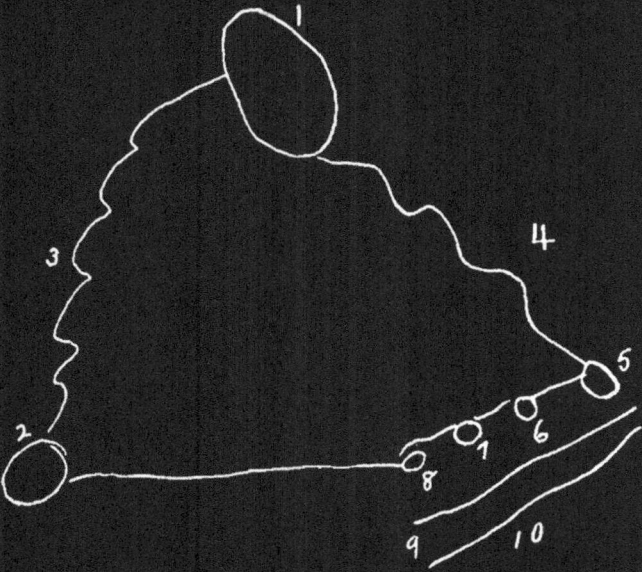

(Kazoola / Langdon Roche 1914, 88)

Inversions, Continued

A Form That Forms the Norm

Images without layers. Depthless. The anthropological diagram: echoing another time, a century out of date. In the plural, a million variations on a common theme. A collection of canonical relics. There are those that persist, or act in assumed silence, or else re-emerge via their own particular modes of resuscitation, bearing minor modifications. A common ancestor, regularly plotted to be the first, still routinely gets stuck at the top of the tree. Here, too. In the opening paragraphs.

An abstraction for all; the abstract of everyone.

In 1910, William H.R. Rivers published a visualization of kinship in the form of a genealogical diagram (fig. 3.1). Rivers adapted the form to other contexts and it was quickly and widely adopted by his peers. That form became an anthropological method. It is still recognizable in kinship diagrams used today. A form that forms the norm. Still exerting influence, this is the work of recurrent modes. Refashioned, abhorrent. The work of both the dead and the undead, condensed in a singular graphic motif: "Ahistorical abstractions *do things*. The formal forms" (Brinkema 2022, 45, emphasis in original). Anthropological diagrams, as "cultural objects," have variously become standardized icons, methods of intelligibility, or tools that further obscure the

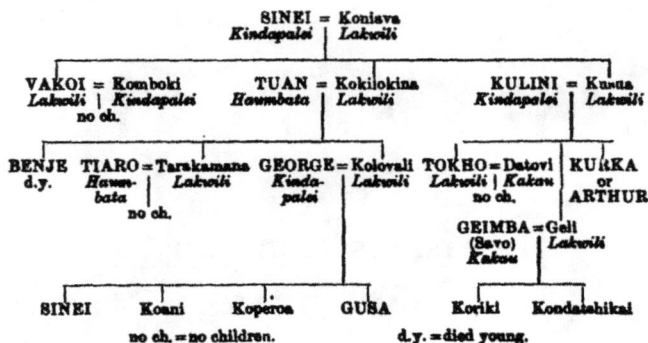

Fig. 3.1. "The Genealogical Method of Anthropological Inquiry" (Rivers 1910, 1).

already complex social relations involved in knowledge generation (Bird-David 2019).

Somewhat in the background of anthropological practice, the use of diagrams has become another "professional model" — like Malinowskian fieldwork — reproducing the discipline without exploring the model's full potential for reflection, creativity, and communication (Grimshaw and Hart 1995, 59, and Mosse 2006). That model persists even while growing numbers of practitioners reject the term "fieldwork" to refer to immersive processes of relationship-building. Disciplines thrive through self-reproduction. Meanwhile, this background positioning of diagrams reflects their disciplinary invisibility: discussion of diagrams has practically never formed a central conversation or recognized sub-focus within anthropology (Lynteris 2017). Persistently present, routinely overlooked. Other visual modes and methods in anthropology have been studied for how they influence disciplinary debates and ideas, a rote step in trying to think beyond inherited dogma, a basic cradle for acting according to a shared critical agenda or embodying the necessity of *kairos*-driven scholarship. The same cannot be said of diagrams, however, despite their origins.

Aspiring after authority. Early use of diagrams explicitly supported positivistic intellectual pursuits and approaches incompatible with critical reflexive practice (Stocking 1992). Deploying situated notions of universality, since justifiably declared unfit. Long dead but never dead. For Rivers, diagrams were about credibility: a means of presenting "facts" in the emergent discipline of ethnology "with as much definiteness as is possible in any biological science" (Rivers 1910, 11–12). Habits die hard. Debates get left behind, but then circle back around. Diagrams are not only analytic or explanatory devices, they also play a generative role in the relationships between ideas and forces, intervening in those processes as agents themselves and as tools wielded by others (Eisenman 2010, 95). Never neutral. The terms change, certain problems remain.

It wasn't always like this; it's often just the same. Grappling with these histories pivots around a point of refusal, not denial. Refusing what Ryan Jobson called a "fictive separation" — the imaginary that separates anthropology as "a space of bourgeois academic work" from "the material histories" that created, formalized, and globally imposed particular disciplinary and imperial practices, now known collectively as "the human sciences" (Jobson 2020, 261). Anthropologists were not mere observers of those processes, they were participants. And what is human about those sciences? Typically, the *human* in that formulation is an impoverished, exclusionary notion of the human — a notion whose dimensions became formalized both physically and metaphysically.

Following Fredric Jameson and others, such processes of formalization create the "prison-house" of (a visual) language: advancing after the prestige of science, then returning to familiar themes with a predefined, symbolic logic, then insisting on recognizable concrete units — combined, these are the tools of any dominant epistemic trade (Jameson 1974). Stuck, outmoded. It is impossible to *erase* the past, but should such tools now be deliberately abandoned, and visual methods and practices reoriented accordingly? Or, can figurative burning be practiced so as to mirror regenerative burning, enabling the current moment to become one in which to reconsider how diagrams could operate *otherwise*? What else might diagrams represent, how, why, and for whom? In place of different depictions of difference, why not novel conceptualizations of interconnection (Partridge 2015)? Images for the formation and dynamism of relationships, imaginations, and possibility. The diagram interpreted as a sign, not yet saturated, not overdetermined. Diagrams read with reference to the conditions of their creation (Davies and Parrinder 2004). In these ways, diagrams have quasi-archaeological potential — a tool to use in unearthing epistemic trends, in tracing and undermining dominant perspectives, and in dismantling and expanding some of the many unfinished, contested histories of anthropological ideas.

Diverse readings, reflecting a multiplicity of perspectives. Refusing any assumed unity of either image or interpretation, whether or not it is or was intended or demanded, by an author or their acolytes. Refusing fictive disciplinary narratives. The refusal is regenerative.

New images — and new imaginaries — emerge from a broader palette of strategies. Those strategies might focus primarily on creativity, (counter)representation, direct action, or all three simultaneously: "The function of any ideology in power is to represent the world positively unified. To challenge the regimes of representation that govern a society is to conceive of how a politics can transform reality rather than merely ideologize it" (Minh-ha 1991, 2). Diagrams simultaneously create and confront this challenge. Not only are diagrams inherently thematically reductive, they are also formally obedient: creating, following, and replicating their own rules. Diagrams are usually drawn using a limited selection of colors and components, operating through "an internal reduction of each of those elements... governed by a unity of image" (Brinkema 2022, 212). The violence of unification. An abstracted, mirror-image of forced assimilation. Synthesis is the inverse of reductive violence.

Meanwhile, the inverse aspect of coherence is correspondence. The synthetic allows multiple ideas to cohere within a singular frame. When multiple frames correspond to one another, a shared visual language emerges. Visualizations of kinship — the relations supporting social structure and continuity — repeat that synthetic view. The result is the formalizing form of the kinship diagram. To rethink the potential of diagrams as visual devices, exploring multiple visual languages, we need to look elsewhere.

Outside of anthropology, diagrams or "theory pictures" have been assessed in broader terms regarding their capacity to illustrate, exemplify, or support written arguments (Lynch 1991, 19). A typical definition emphasizes how each diagram restructures the terms of its own interpretation: "the idea of a diagram, or pattern, is very simple. It is an abstract pattern of physical relationships which resolves a small system of interacting and conflicting forces, and is independent of all other forces, and of all other possible diagrams" (Alexander 1979, v). The idea of latent potential remains key. Brian Massumi partially referenced the Deleuzian *abstract diagram* (as I discuss in Part IV, "Diagrams to Discomfort") in their description of how we might decipher the stasis of diagrams, a process that can be applied to identifying the possibilities and potentialities they contain: "Diagramming is the procedure of abstraction when it is not concerned with reducing the world to an aggregate of objects but, quite the opposite, when it is attending to their genesis [...] extracting the relational-qualitative arc of one occasion of experience and systematically depositing it in the world for the next occasion to find [...] the activity of formation appearing stilled" (Massumi 2011, 14, 99). Massumi's approach was a point of departure for initial versions of this work re-thinking histories of diagrams in anthropology (Partridge 2014). And the possibilities that Massumi invokes generate a central question for exploring the visual potential of diagrams within anthropology: are there ways to see social connections complementary to the experience of living, embodying, and describing those connections?

In part, this means reconsidering how diagrams in anthropology have emerged and how else we might engage with, understand, or critique those trajectories. There is more to the visual work of Rivers, for example, than the violence of imposed scientific order. Anna Grimshaw considers emergent diagrammatic forms to be analogous with Cubist painting: the diagram "shares with modern art an emphasis on flatness" since "pictorial depth or perspective is abandoned; it is made up of a multiplicity of perspectives or viewpoints; it draws attention to the relationships or processes; it does not describe what can be seen, but rather it is an abstract representation which evokes the complexity of the visible" (Grimshaw 2001, 40). In this sense, such visual methods are diagrammatic in ways that echo the diagrammatic processes of power itself: mobilizing both predefined and ill-defined matter and concepts, unfolding through contested modes of reception, and ultimately subject to its own flexibility (Deleuze 1988, 73). The act of rendering connections visible remains open to redefinition.

Those definitions have changed over time. The invisibility of diagrams in anthropology is relative. There are anthropological works that critically assess the history and development of diagrams (e.g., Engelmann, Humphrey, and Lynteris 2019), but within the discipline as a whole these assessments remain somewhat peripheral, especially in comparison with the relative centrality, familiarity, and prevalence of diagrams themselves. There are scholars who suggest that diagrams bring an efficiency of expression to anthropological texts as well as the capacity to convey information in non-linear ways (Banks 2001). Such claims are often countered, however, by those who note that diagrams are usually intelligible only when explained by some accompanying text — thus rendering the visual elements more of an indulgence than an effective way of tightening the delivery of information (Candea 2019). Seeking out the synthetic, the coherent, the singular, each example and iteration adds to a growing corpus that cannot avoid inviting further examples through cross-correspondences. Each recognizable contribution is an echo of an original form: "The starting point of synthesis is the diagram. The end product of synthesis is the realization of the problem, which is a tree of diagrams" (Alexander 1979, 84). Branch after branch, the genealogies stick, the offspring proliferate. Raised above the parapets — in fact, there to watch over the discipline's own imagined borders — the most visible is the most examined. Extant critiques and (re)assessments of diagrams in anthropology have focused mainly on the most commonly encountered kind: kinship diagrams.

The Framework Sets the Limits / The Limits Are the Framework

What are these schematic assemblages of complex social worlds? What work are they doing? Tim Ingold questions the inherent "decontextualising linearity" of kinship diagrams — each of which presents a sterile "snapshot" of relations stripped of their biographies and interactions (Ingold 2000, 140). Pierre Bourdieu describes them as counterintuitive depictions of human connection; images in which the flow of time is disrupted and time itself becomes artificially concentrated. Each diagram may show an extensive network of kinship relations, spanning several generations, but those relations are presented as only "theoretical objects" and the network as a "totality present in simultaneity" (Bourdieu 1977, 38). Time and connections collapse into the analytical plane, as do their protagonists: "the graphic is a diagram when the correspondences on the plane can be established among all the elements of one component and all the elements of *another* component. [...This is the] process of construction: in order to *construct* a diagram, it is necessary: (a) to determine a form of representation for the components; [and] (b) to record the correspondences" (Bertin 2010, 193, emphasis in original). The violence of the assumption: the exclusion of meaning in order to achieve universality.

Mary Bouquet examines affinities between "European iconographical traditions in sacred, secular and scientific family trees" and the "conceptual field" that supported the development of the anthropological kinship diagram (Bouquet 1996, 45, 59). The process predates the work of Rivers. In addition to religious and scientific precursors, Lewis Henry Morgan's "diagrams of consanguinity" in his *Systems of Consanguinity and Affinity of the*

See Page 32. DIAGRAM OF CONSANGUINITY: ENGLISH. PLATE III.

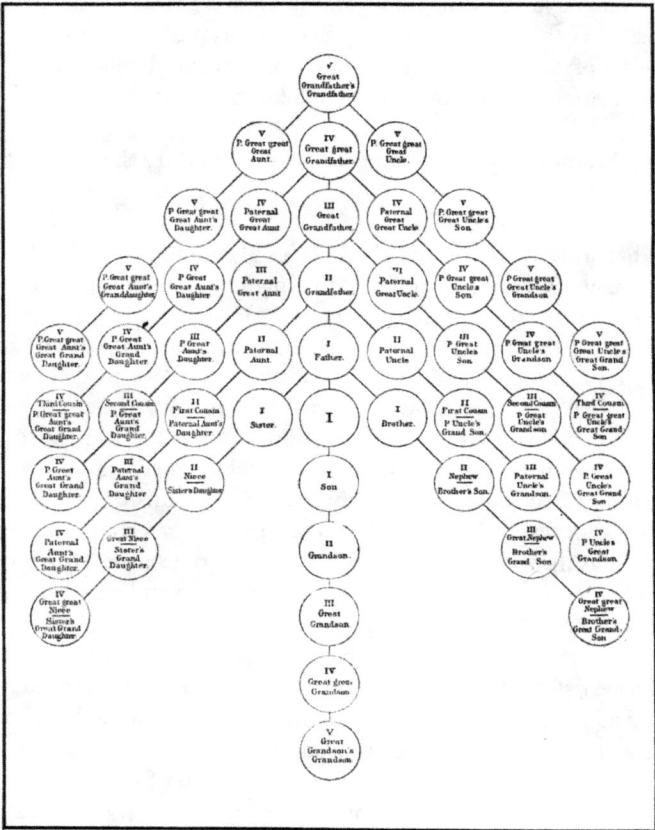

Fig. 3.2. One of Morgan's (1871) "diagrams of consanguinity." Modeled after: British Records (1841) Commission Series, *Ancient Laws and Institutes of Wales,* book XI, ch. IV, p. 605.

Human Family (1871) were also based on historical models of the "family tree" (fig. 3.2).

But Rivers explicitly brought the diagram into the center of the research process, arguing that the systematic presentation of genealogical information connected individuals to the relations they were born into and developed throughout their lifetime, helping to identify and give a sense of biography for even those who were distant in terms of geography or generation (Bouquet 1996; Rivers 1910). There is a reinforcing circularity at play here. The content of diagrams displays names gathered through "concrete methods" and fieldwork conversations, while the diagrammatic form that connects those names forms an "abstract system" that can be adapted and applied to other contexts — but that abstract order is then "reconcretized" by being visualized in each specific genealogical diagram (Bouquet 1996, 45).

Rivers's diagrams contributed further to the conventionalization of inverting the *tree* of family trees: the ancestors are elevated, the direction of "descent" is reinforced, and the tree grows downward from the roots (Bouquet 1995 Watson 1934). The abstraction, deepened. The image of the tree as a living entity is replaced with a geometric code assembled from dots (each of which is a person) and lines (each of which is a connection) (Ingold 2000, 135). Each geometrical line is a "ghost" of an actual trace, movement, experience, or thread (Ingold 2007, 111). The abstraction, achieved: a visual language capable of codifying any or all peoples and their relationships, that code intelligible to readers perhaps completely unfamiliar with the diagram's content or context. Further inversions followed. Multiplicities were made singular. Disembodied, godlike views from nowhere prevailed: "By the second decade of the twentieth century [...] science and reason, appropriated in the names of democracy, were now strategies of control employed by the agents of state power. The anxious, fragmented, multiperspectival modernist vision of Rivers is transformed into 'the gaze,' the disembodied eye of observation. [...] Society is 'observed' and turned into an object to be studied" (Grimshaw 2001, 67). The consequences of visual work for anthropological method, and the implications of visual work as method, reflected back immediately on the scientistic pretensions of anthropological work that pursued and relied upon universalizing forms of abstraction.

The diagram is a container for thought. A visual reflection of the discourse of the day. Again this is the "prison-house" of dis-

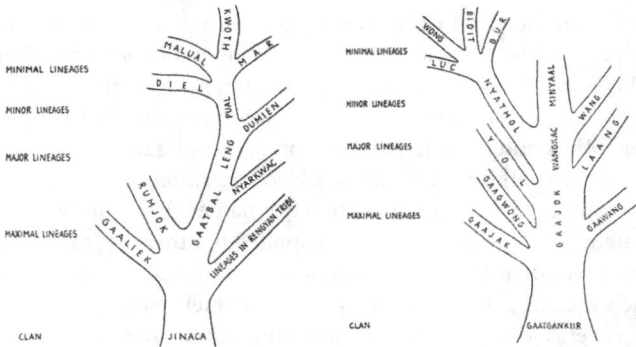

Fig. 3.3. Evans-Pritchard's (1940, 196–97) diagrammatic lineage trees of the Jinaca (left) and Gaatgankiir (right).

ciplinary visuality: the invention of symbolic logics and subsequent insistence on their use in studying discrete, concrete, isolated units of analysis. Anthropology witnessed and facilitated the spread of methodological practices that deny a plurality of experiential or cognitive modes for both visualizing theory and theorizing visuality (Taylor 1994). The reductive mapping of cultural life, the flattening of cross-cultural experience within atemporal metaphors — metaphors that mask an otherwise rich world of sensory encounters (Seremetakis 1993). Diagrams are all these things, do all these things, differentially. The genealogical diagram is a case in point, reflecting the limits of a disciplinary, ideological consciousness (Bouquet 1996). The framework sets the limits; the limits are the framework. Diagramming the conceptual points beyond which disciplinary consciousness is disinclined to go — the points between which the discipline is destined to self-oscillate (Jameson 1981). The result? A shared language restricting its own communicative powers and potentialities.

At certain times within the histories of anthropology, however, the inter-relationship of method and visuality has generated moments of formal variation, even if these variations remained momentary and did little to unseat the persistent presence of genealogical diagrams.

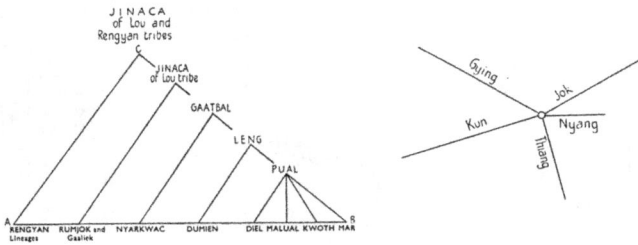

Fig. 3.4. Left: Evans-Pritchard's (1940, 201) outline of a Nuer system of lineage. Right: "How the Nuer themselves figure a lineage system" (1940, 202).

There have been occasional flexes to the visual language that emerged through experimentation, some variations in design and orientation that reflected contemporaneous intellectual endeavors. Anthropology's obsessions, drawn, and drawn out. Theoretical, disciplinary conceptions of kinship were central to anthropology's preoccupation with the social organization of small-scale, effectively state-less societies (shared among Bronislaw Malinowski, A.R. Radcliffe-Brown, Edward Evans-Pritchard, Meyer Fortes, and many others), a focus that fueled ahistorical studies of kinship structures like lineages, sublineages, etc. and a fixation on evermore complex *typologies* of relationships (Carsten 2004). The governing influence of these typologies is clear in Evans-Pritchard's diagrams that depict notions of scale in the inter-relationships between Nuer communities and lineages — hierarchical connections between (sub) lineages give shape to each drawn image and their differently-sized branches — adopting another visual metaphor of the tree to relay this information (fig. 3.3).

Evans-Pritchard further made attempts to represent Nuer people with descriptions and depictions of these inter-relationships (fig. 3.4).

In these attempts, he explicitly states that it was only the analyst (whom he calls "we") who insisted on the use of particular visual metaphors, highlighting some of the limitations of those routine metaphors: "[the Nuer] do not present [lineages]

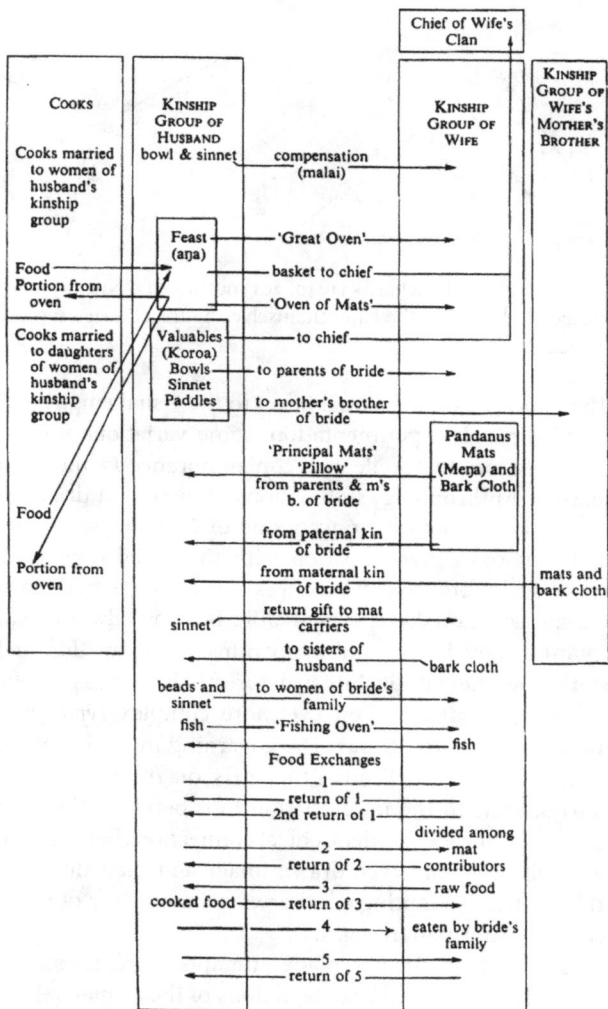

Fig. 3.5. Lévi-Strauss (1969, 64) draws on Firth (1939) to highlight the "astonishing complexity of matrimonial exchanges in Tikopia" (Solomon Islands), cementing relations between specific groups of "in-laws" and binding each lineage (or kinship group) in "a system of directional exchanges."

the way we figure them as a series of bifurcations of descent, as a tree of descent, or as a series of triangles of ascent, but as a number of lines running at angles from a common point... they see [the system] as actual relations between groups of kinsmen within local communities rather than as a tree of descent, for the persons after whom the lineages are called do not all proceed from a single individual" (Evans-Pritchard 1940, 202).

Disciplinary tensions of the era between tools of visualization and interpretation — either those with their origins in the analyst's preconceptions, or those stemming from people's descriptions of their own conceptual universe — were not the only source of diagrammatic experimentation and development.

During this era of kinship studies in Britain, analytical preoccupations focused on "descent groups" while such projects in France followed a route influenced by Claude Lévi-Strauss's *The Elementary Structures of Kinship* (1969), with an emphasis instead on social rules, the generation of exchange, and marriage (Carsten 2004, 12). The once-raging debates between adherents of "alliance" or "descent" theories do not need to be repeated here. Of note, however, is the increasing complexity of diagrams used in those debates. Lévi-Strauss's focus on how relations were established and maintained between groups — rather than just between individuals — saw him develop elaborate, diagrammatic models for the exchange of goods and services over time (Carsten 2004, 14). Alfred Gell (1999, 31) centers the work of Lévi-Strauss when making the point that the "heyday of structuralism" was marked by "excesses of diagramming." Modernism at large, another modernism at work. Visual expressions of work that fashions tools to fashion subjects, and vice versa. Closing the interpretive loop.

The excess of being comprehensive. Excessive attempts to render complexity within two dimensions. Many of the Lévi-Strauss images are inscrutable, complex to a point where any economy of expression that might be achieved visually is lost (fig. 3.5). However, the structure and arrangement of this particular example — divided into two interconnected spaces representing

kinship groups — does closely match this diagram's purposive
content, namely to represent the view that relations between
specific groups are cemented through exchanges. Forcing the
form to fit. A relic-endeavor, of its time. Bourdieu's critique of
kinship diagrams applies also to such approaches to structuring images, questioning constructed views of kin relationships
that either (a) reproduce an official representation of social
structures and the functioning of legitimating processes within
a given social order, or (b) create representations that are produced by the application of a "structuring principle" (Bourdieu
1977, 34). In this sense, it is an inversion of the original modernist impulse seen in the work of Rivers: that impulse looked to
reduce the world to an abstract form but did so in order to construct a more complex view of reality, looking not only beyond
realism in representations and reproductions, but also beyond
the idea of single, solid, stable, visible *reality* (Grimshaw 2001,
37). The Lévi-Strauss example (1969, 64) instead becomes lost
within its own reality, an utterance so committed to its goal of
structuring the potential that it becomes relatively unrelatable.

Hence the inversion: rather than exploring what Grimshaw
(2001, 67) describes as the "anxious, fragmented, multiperspectival modernist vision" to see more complex realities, the Lévi-
Strauss example instead creates a more complex view of abstraction. The excessive potential of an abstract form, pursued with
such commitment, becomes its own undoing. If this is a cau-
tionary tale, then the question is: What would it take to reverse
this inversion? What, if any, potential remains in that modernist
drive to expand realities via visual abstractions?

Diagrams as Stories, Diagrams as Models

Support for the suitability of diagrams as a non-textual form
of presenting anthropological material has come from multiple canonical sources: phrased in terms of their adaptability as
models for social relations (Barnard and Good 1984); as offering
synoptic bases for comparison (Malinowski 1922); or phrased in
terms of cognition (Gell 1999). In this last sense, Gell suggests

are contained or depicted in the diagram, offer crucial insight and examples both for comparison with exchange relations in other contexts and for revising theoretical frameworks.

A diagram's graphic form is embedded in relationships with what is conveyed in written text. Diagrams themselves often feature words and terms specific to the field of analysis. To *read* a diagram is thus to approach it as an "intermediate configuration at once visual and lexical" (Conley 2011, 165). Reading mathematical or geometric diagrams similarly involves interpreting the information they synthesize and, in the process, discerning relations between elements that previously and in other contexts appear to share no necessary connection (Peirce 1931). Charles Sanders Peirce describes diagrams as the "hypostatization" or reification of relations. Reading diagrams means regarding the abstract in a concrete form — but also looking beyond resemblance to analogy. Diagrams can represent the relations that connect parts of one thing with analogous relations between the image's own constituent parts (Adams 1996). Reading diagrams is the act of interpreting such resemblances, relations, and analogies. Genealogical diagrams model social relations, portraying the inter-relationships of individuals both present and absent (Barnard and Good 1984, 8). The *significance* of such diagrams, though, is not established until "the nature of those relationships between the individuals portrayed is clarified" (Bouquet 1996, 45). Expectations are low. The visual, a minimal guide. Very little is demanded of the diagram — text always completes the picture.

Explanatory text also serves to clarify whether the diagram-as-model *fits* or *guides*. The "fit" is evocative, the "guide" an intervention. A "model of reality" describes an observed phenomenon, interaction, or regularity rather than claiming any "reality of the model" which, like a map, would govern, direct, or orient behavior around knowable or recognizable phenomena (Bourdieu 1990, 39). Clifford Geertz outlines a parallel clarification of the term *model* in reference to "cultural patterns" and more comprehensive cultural systems, one small part of which would usually be the subject of a single diagram. A "model of" charts physical relationships so as to "render them apprehensible" (for example establishing how a dam works through theories of hydraulics and flow charts), while a "model for" provides a basis for guiding and organizing physical relationships (for example constructing a dam according to those prior theories and charts) (Geertz 1973, 93).

As audience-members, we are more likely to encounter images and models that refer to unfamiliar contexts and narratives, and so most diagrams operate as models of — offering explanatory snapshots — rather than the definitive, comprehensive maps that constitute models for. Visual conventions can facilitate the process of rendering new contexts apprehensible (Partridge, 2025). Many diagrams do this in one form or another, for example by using arrows to denote directional flow or movement. But the distinction here between of and for is not always absolute. Diagrams that offer a general model of, for example, reciprocal exchange (such as those in Sahlins 1972) are in many ways prospective, illustrating the *potential* for certain kinds of interaction to take place or certain relations to form, be tested, be strengthened, or dissolve. In this sense, such diagrams simultaneously resemble a model for, a guide, were we to find ourselves located at some physical point or situation within the diagram or suggested by it.

The content of diagrams as models of — continuums, combinations, spectrums, conjunctions — is far from arbitrary (Deleuze and Guattari 1987, 71). Each choice reflects relations between the components of an image and relations within the conditions of its creation. In this light, diagrams can be considered "iconic" (resembling the object or objects they relate to), "indexical" (affected by their object or objects, in the sense of being dependent on their stories to convey any information), and "symbolic" (aided by visual conventions) at the same time — thus both drawing on and reinforcing disciplinary modes of communication (Adams 1996, and Peirce 1931). Those modes might be visual conventions, such as the circles and triangles of kinship diagrams, or more theoretical, such as how Evans-Pritchard's tree diagrams above were drawn to accom-

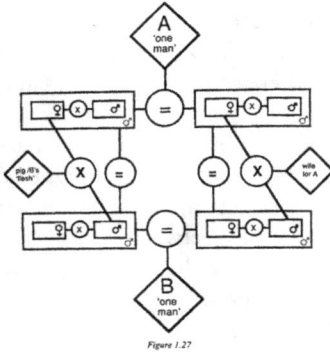

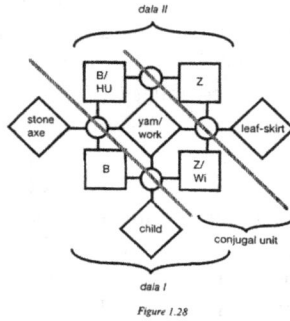

Fig. 3.7. Left: an "impossible figure" to reflect the symbolic practices of marriage and affinity (Gell 1999, 64). Right: another "Strathernogram" from Gell (1999, 72) detailing the specific working and feeding relations that constitute and support the *dala*.

modate an intellectual focus on maximal and minimal lineages. Other explorations of the potential of diagrams in anthropology have deliberately constructed modes of their own.

One such invented mode was conceived as a "thought experiment" to express complex theoretical inferences in a visual plane, without relying on outside conventions. Gell (1999) developed a unique graphic system to represent "system M" — the "Melanesia" that became a focus of anthropological discourse, as primarily articulated in Marilyn Strathern's (1988) *The Gender of the Gift:* "an account of the social world based on the premises that the social world consists of relationships between terms, and is thus ideal, and that the perceptible world consists of appearances which encypher the social world" (Gell 1999, 36). Within this graphic system, terms (all of which are gendered) are in rectangular or square boxes, relations (all of which are exchange relations) are in circles or ovals, and appearances or real-world things are placed in lozenges or diamonds.

In the first example of Gell's "Strathernograms" (fig. 3.7), we find interlinked, codified nominal and symbolic elements arranged to reflect the symbolic practices of marriage and affinity within "system M." These practices are dependent on "cross/ sex unmediated and same/sex mediated 'readings' of gendered exchanges" — at the root of conflict between alliance theory and feminist critiques (Gell 1999, 64).

The model derives from the fact that "any Melanesian marriage is both collective and individual," unlike what might be a more familiar stipulation that "relations are *either* between individuals (interpersonal/private) *or* between collectivities (corporate/public)" (Gell 1999, 63, emphasis in original). Since individual and society are not opposed, the "relationship between marriage (the union between specific spouses) and alliance (affinal alliance linking collectivities such as clans) can be understood in terms of fractal magnification/minimization": an approximate, but not exact, analogy between "spouse-to-spouse relations and affinal-group to affinal-group relations" (Gell 1999, 63). In the second example, Gell outlines the specific working and feeding relations that constitute and support the *dala:* a matrilineal sub-community described as the "enduring, self-reproducing, building-blocks of Trobriand society" (Gell 1999, 70–72).

In some respects, these diagrams are merely a proof of concept — meeting the challenge of rendering complex social relations in visual form using a specially-constructed visual lexicon. However, just as Jablonko's diagram illustrates not only past, observed encounters but also potential, future interactions that would likely occur at a given point in the corresponding physical world, so does Gell's thought experiment — which he admits "ineluctibly bears the impress" of western concepts and assumptions against which it is constructed — offer "imaginings" that illuminate "what the world might look like, seen from a counter-intuitive point of view" (Gell 1999, 74). However, if any such "abstract system" is to "generate insights" into parts of the data from which it is constructed — and to bolster knowledge claims made on that basis — it still always has to be "aligned with ethnography" (Gell 1999, 74). The constant partner to images and diagrams: detailed, explanatory text.

IV

Excess (Possibilities)

Commonality Denied

Diagrams are working objects: they emerge *through work* as "both the tools and products of research processes," and they *do work* by plotting correlations between familiar oppositions of word or image, representation or reality, ideas or objects, vision or interpretation (Bender and Marrinan 2010, 10). Working objects are not full concepts or theories. They are instead some of the materials that are used to give shape and presence to concepts — "manageable representatives" of a topic or focus of investigation (Daston and Galison 1992). Engelmann, Humphrey, and Lynteris (2019) highlight how in anthropological research not all diagrams are used to simplify, schematize, or standardize information, nor are they limited to illustrating research findings. This is in contrast to other diagrams, especially those that serve singular purposes or are constructed and disseminated in relative isolation: "A diagram is its form. Nothing before, nothing after, nothing outside: it is solely its arrangement of elements." Its "form cannot be modified without it becoming a different form, which is to say: another diagram altogether" (Brinkema 2022, 232). Working *with* these working objects can give diagrams a more unpredictable, often ephemeral, role within the processes of observation, analysis, and theorizing that constitute the work of research and writing (Engelmann, Humphrey, and Lynteris 2019). Diagrams do not only exist, or function, as products. Often, they are also a formative part of the *doing* of research.

Diagrams are shaped by the roles they play in broader networks. They are embedded in a poetic tradition that sees voice and graphic form ruptured, re-placed, and brought back together in new collisions of thought (Conley 2011, 165). Diagrams are a crucible in which aesthetic and epistemic elements interact. Variously reflecting, challenging, or replicating disciplinary modes and models, these interactions facilitate the creation of new visual-lexical configurations.

Diagrams form a visual hub for concentric histories of design and imagination. They foreground the "outside" of thought — or what cannot be put into language — by closing a circle that connects the aesthetic, the textual, and the non-lexical (Conley 2011, 165). Despite operating as an abstraction, diagrams do not necessarily share the timelessness of the abstract (though they typically do). Often a diagram also acts as an author's intervention in wider epistemic processes — as discussed with reference to Edward Evans-Pritchard and Claude Lévi-Strauss in Part III — or as an intentional comment on the relationship between knowledge creation and visual culture (Eddy 2014, 179). Diagrams emerge from within this tension between poetic-aesthetic tradition and contemporary-discursive commentary. Part of our *reading* of diagrams involves tracing how evident such processes are: whether or how the visual tools used rely on shared conditions and traditions, or how explicitly academic precursors, debates, and audience-members are addressed. This tension further highlights the connection that diverse diagrams in anthropology hold with their common origin: fieldwork experiences. The vitality of those experiences — embodied, emotional, expressive, relational — lies in contrast to the two-dimensionality of the textual products that anthropology uses in order to analyze and describe them. Where is the human, where are the humans?

Descriptions in the present tense tend to create a sense of perpetuity, stability, and stasis. Behavior in general, as well as the multiple specific interactions that constitute any one form or sphere of action, are artificially held in place. The desire to comprehend action leads to the attempt to contain it, as if actions could be either containable and comprehensible within any one moment or representation. The implication being not only that such actions can be traced but also that, in their traceability, such actions are predictable and replicable (Sanjek 1991, 612). The partial present. The present tense without tension. A once-present moment captured and described but soon lost to the absence of presence that surrounds that description. An observation lacking sufficient context. A statement made without embodiment. A reflection subsequently blurred between other, overlapping reflections, each with their own origin, destination, and source of light. A comment for nobody. A hall-of-mirrors utterance. These are the findings of note.

The distancing of diagrams.

Artificially split apart, kept separate. A common wall dissolved.

The ethnographic present communicates a perspective that imagines human action as conventional and governed by rules. This same imagination, however, sees the world of writing and knowledge-creation very differently — as practices based on situational influences, able to maintain a sense of their own contingency and intentionality (Sanjek 1991, 612). Such an imagined distinction — or distancing — between processes and products of knowledge creation calls into question the particular relationships of observation and inquiry that underpin those processes (Hastrup 1990). The subsequent formulation of different representations then reflects back, again, on those same processes of generation.

Pierre Bourdieu marks the *linearity* of diagrams as susceptible to precisely this error of distancing, including the diagrams he constructed to depict seasonal shifts in local activity and organization during the agrarian year in Kabylia (fig. 4.1).

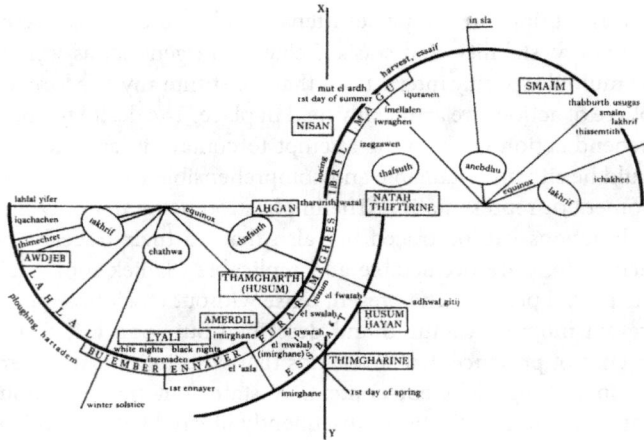

Fig. 2. The abstract "calendar"

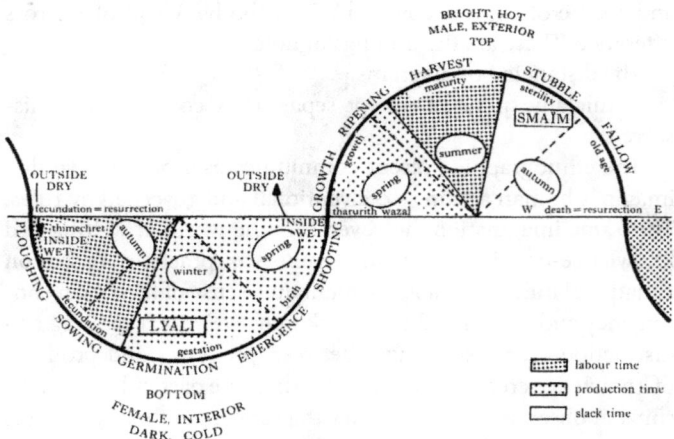

Fig. 3. The farming year and the mythical year

Fig. 4.1. Two of five sine-wave diagrams (Bourdieu 1977, 99, 134). Top: the abstract "calendar." Bottom: the farming year and the mythical year (bottom).

He describes these diagrams as an attempt to systematically accumulate and "fix" a successive flow of actions and relations into one simultaneous image (Bourdieu 1977, 104–5). He also notes that, in creating these diagrams, the contradictions that emerge between life-as-lived and its momentary representation are at once masked and revealed — not only do new tensions emerge between one temporal instance and others before and since, but the institutional tendency to bury such gaps and tensions is also cast in a new light (Bourdieu 1977). The argument runs that such practices of institutional "objectification" themselves need to be turned into objects of reflection — to become the subject of scrutiny in order to more effectively question the *operations* or processes that give rise to subsequent texts, images, and knowledge objects (Bourdieu 1977, 106). The *operative* merely precedes the representative. Each is retrospectively defined. The many ways of transcribing and translating experience are folded into singular channels of communication.

Detemporalized Relationships, Performative Rationality

The ready critiques: gaze, time, orientation, and reduction.

Diagrams draw attention to some of the political implications of apparently methodological, epistemological problems — the inevitable tensions between the endless flow of experience and the momentary confines of representation. Diagrams reflect views on validity in which knowledge is conceived as the "reproduction of an observed world," part of a broader "political cosmology" that defines relationships of observation in temporal terms (Fabian 2014, 87). Coherence is a betrayal.

These are not new concerns. Antoine Augustin Cournot (1922, 364) contrasts spoken or written discourse, as a succession of signs expressing relationships that the mind can perceive in a given order, with "synoptic" images, such as diagrams and family trees, which utilize lines and text across their surface so as to "represent systematic relations and links which it would be difficult to make out in the flow of discourse" (Bourdieu 1977, 221). Everyday life is a flow of practices that are "detotalized" by virtue of being emergent within the "current of time" (Bourdieu 1977, 221). The construction of a diagram transforms and *totalizes* that flow of practices by drawing into a single space only a fraction of possible relationships, while at the same time also populating that space with more elements than could be simultaneously "mobilized together" in actual practice: this tension simply underscores how everyday life is far more urgent and messy than the "internal coherence" that most diagrams suggest (Bourdieu 1977, 9, 106). Coherence makes too much sense: the construction of an impossible order.

Diagrams depict relationships that are detemporalized, taken out of the flow of time that gives them character and specificity, presenting them as "logical relationships" that exist as types, as opposed to "practical relationships" that are continuously "practiced and cultivated" in flesh-and-blood settings (Bourdieu 1977, 37–38). Diagrams become maps of a kind, only without a singular intention to lead. Diagrammatic space is filled with detemporalized relationships, a flat dehumanized version of the world it represents, just as the "geometrical space of a map, an imaginary representation of all theoretically possible roads and routes, is opposed to the network of beaten tracks, of paths made ever more practicable by constant use" (Bourdieu 1977, 37–38).

Temporally, diagrams are distancing devices: one form of many such existential, discursive, rhetorical, and political devices that are built into anthropological practice. All such devices deepen the divide between fieldwork, intersubjectivity, and ethical accountability on one hand, and representation on the other. This distancing goes beyond the *atemporality* of modes of expression dependent on the present tense (Fabian 2014). Distancing devices reinforce anthropology's "allochronic" orientation, a fictive and violent separation of observer and observed, a denial of "coevalness" seen in the "persistent and systematic tendency to place the referent(s) of anthropology in a Time other than the present of the producer of anthropological discourse" (Fabian 2014, 31). Ideologies of Othering are built upon the denial of shared time. The apparent atemporality of diagrams — whether the result of fixing a social world in time, or of abstracting social relations to types — runs counter to the dynamism and polyphony of the lives and experiences they represent.

Diagrams organize and present information in ways that are both highly selective (disregarding some relations) and reductive (condensing empirical complexity into clear, more limited, images). If anthropology usually aims at a dialogic process of making knowledge out of shared experience, then diagrams appear as antithetical icons (Fabian 1990; Hastrup 2004). Feminist frameworks for participatory research have for a long time drawn attention to the importance of making any editorial selections explicit — recognizing that the choices of voices, the foregrounding of certain perspectives or ideas over others, is a fundamental dynamic both within the research process itself (Maguire 1987, 5) and in the presentation stages of research (Reid 2004, 4). The performative order, the meticulousness, the ostentatiousness of diagrams run counter to this focus. Even practitioners who used diagrams were — rightly — suspicious of the work these reductive images perform, including Bourdieu (1990, 85): "Nothing is more suspect than the ostentatious rigour of so many diagrams of social organization offered by anthropologists." In their personal correspondence, Marilyn Strathern similarly commented to Alfred Gell that diagrams can be used in questionable ways, specifically to give a "spurious logic to texts which are, in fact, discursively incoherent" (Gell 1999, 31). Even outside of overtly scientist pretensions — Diagrams Display Facts — the use of diagrams is often read as being performative, signaling seriousness.

Handling diagrams in anthropology connects to other methodological, ethical, and political concerns across the discipline as a whole. Specifically, it connects to that fundamental practice: the construction of anthropological texts. Knowledge produced through fieldwork research is "shaped, if not determined" by the forms of writing, reading, and approaches to representation that the author adopts (Parkin 2000, 91). Diagrams almost epitomize the power imbalances inherent in the process of "writing up" when it is seen as an "opportunity to impose a retrospective order on a set of often-disordered events and impressions" (Hannabuss 2000, 101). Ordering through distancing.

Diagrams have no place for disorder. The abstract only emerges once life's messiness has been removed, the excess excised.

Similarly, ethnographic writing is at its most misleading when it echoes that diagrammatic dynamic, using "analytical abstraction to tidy, and thus claim authority over, messy realities" (Lenhard and Samanani 2020, 19). At the same time, however, reflexive critique and practice have highlighted such tendencies to mislead, exposed the authoritative motivations that lie behind them, and have pushed ethnographic writing toward other, more exploratory ends. Do diagrams have a role to play in further exploring expansive modes of knowledge (co)creation? It would seem hasty to declare it impossible to imagine any visual form that might construct and share knowledge otherwise. Also persistent is the potential for visual forms to "engage productively with the messy surplus of life: the excess of historical interconnections, varied perspectives and shifting subjectivities that resist[ed] neat containment within singular, authoritative texts" (Lenhard and Samanani 2020, 19). Anticipating disorder, committing to confusion. Stories won't tell themselves. The role of diagrams becomes one of expanding our engagements with the multiple and the many — additional aspects to reflect and reflect on both anthropological ideas and source materials.

Potentiality, Surplus, and Possibilities Not Yet Explored

Marc Augé describes "anthropological space" as more than merely an "assembly of elements coexisting in a certain order" — as a diagrammatic image might depict — and instead as a space that also includes the discourses, language, and possible journeys made in and through it, elements which animate a particular place and which, in turn, give rise to the experiences of people moving and interacting within it (Augé 1995, 81). Narrativizing such journeys of doing and seeing becomes the basis of ethnographic text and representations. However, the flow of experience exceeds representation. Not all journeys and actions, not all forms of doing, being, and seeing are "reducible" to a state of being recognized as knowledge or knowledge-objects (Jackson 1996, 3). Anthropological fieldwork continually reveals a surplus. More moments than could ever be catalogued. More voices than would ever be heard.

Anthropological diagrams are both borne of and suggestive of the surplus. The many constituent parts of this historical surplus (events, thoughts, ideas, and acts) cannot all be identified or mapped. Diagrams are images "on the edge of the text" (Stoller 1992, 56). Referents always echo a relatively unidentified and unmapped space beyond the text, beyond representation — a manifold realm that exists beyond frames and frameworks. It is within this multiplicity that new spaces of possibility emerge as potential "sites of resistance" or "new historical turns" (Hastrup 2004, 461). The surplus is possibility.

Echoing Michel de Certeau (1984), what appears as a static diagram, which appears to display only an inventory of identifiable points and characters, still also contains the possibility of other journeys into and through that space, the possibility of routes not taken or not yet taken (Augé 1995, 81). In contrast to the "excess of meaning" of statistical knowledge, which makes knowledge claims about both stated objects and generalizations for similar cases elsewhere, anthropological knowledge is carved from the "excess of experience" of social life (Hastrup 2004, 461). Not every possible encounter has been observed, nor every form of interaction experienced, before observations are made. Statements are partial, texts incomplete. Likewise with diagrams: beyond the representational content of its carefully plotted components, the image might more expansively suggest the potential for certain kinds of interactions or events to occur.

Anthropology, however, follows in the footsteps of philosophy and recreates similar errors when it continues to insist that it has the infinite at its disposal, mistaking its own creations as concretized meaning rather than orchestrated theorems (Adorno 1973). The surplus is not always intelligible. The infinite is not equally divided. Limitless diversity is not evenly distributed. The promise of gathering together and ordering an anthropological surplus is perpetually unfulfilled. The insistence on sense-making is perpetual movement, ultimately undirected or circular in its path.

Diagrams recover the chaos of surplus when they are used to reformulate our understandings of the potential. Jon Bialecki (2017) applies Deleuzian (1988) notions of the abstract diagram to the particular dynamics of ethnographic contexts. Here, the diagram is itself a form of understanding: a mode of engaging with (and thinking through) how "abstract relations between social forces [can] be actualized in different modes" and how "the relation between these social forces can be transposed to new spaces and can further play out to different effects" (Bialecki 2017, 20). Notions of the potential, in turn, may respond to changes that occur as a result of transferring information from textual to visual form. As Lynch argues (1991, 19), diagrams are not intended to "resemble observable phenomena" but to create a "hermeneutic space" and a dialogue between "writing and figure."

Diagrams merge the formative and finalized elements of an image. This makes it possible to read diagrams not as simply "pictures of something (or of nothing)" but instead as "armatures in movement" that are completed by, and act in response to, our perceptions and readings (Lynch 1991, 19). This is a double-movement, articulating a language of expression and perception (the suitability and clarity of visual forms) and reflecting the creative processes involved in generating diagrams by drawing both on fieldwork experiences and on prior scholarly work.

This diagrammatic focus on potentiality also extends the temporal terms of (re)presentation. Veena Das suggests that the relation between representations in anthropological texts and the past set of experiences that have shaped them is not necessarily static, so long as our reading of those representations can include possibilities not specified within the texts and images themselves. Anthropological texts are not sealed. They are not "seamless descriptions of norms and practices of the kind that could be rendered as propositional knowledge of the indicative kind — e.g. 'the Nuer believe that…'." There "is no logical connection between representation and the category of the 'past' — provided our notion of the present is deep enough to include not only the actual but also the potential and the eventual" (Das 2012, 60). Adopting this perspective recasts diagrams not as isolated artefacts to be assessed in terms of accuracy or impact but as the products of relational, dialogic processes that invite reflection on how objects of anthropological investigation are identified and discussed.

Through a focus on the potential, the design and interpretation of diagrams becomes part of the process of recognizing how knowledge is gradually incorporated, renewed, and rejected within processes of objectifying anthropological objects themselves (Hastrup 2004, 468). Knowledge objects are not ontologically fixed; they are always emergent within relational research processes, subject to revisions of our notions of the actual and the potential (Hastrup 2004, 468). Of course, this is not limited to anthropological work and concerns. Diagramming is one of many methods of engagement in knowledge co-creation, an illustrative act that involves much more than arranging lines on a page. Diagramming in this sense is rather thought of in more expansive terms, as "a relational co-emergence of matter and thought that enables new potentialities to emerge" (Springgay and Zaliwska 2015, 144). Diagrams can both challenge and extend that sense of emergence — reconnecting via other means different events and experiences, both past and present.

The past is present in more ways than one. Perception is a process, and interpretation its shadow. John Dewey (1934, 24) argues that to see, and to perceive, involves more than merely *recognizing*: we do not identify something present in terms of a "past disconnected from it" nor do we interpret only a succession of "labels" of situations, events, and objects in order to comprehend them. We recognize historical relations of change between those events and objects. Thus "every idea" has "a local habitation" (Dewey 1934, 90): the specific set of circumstances from which it has emerged. These circumstances are unfinished, even in an object or image that is based upon them and is presented as a completed artifact. Every idea is thus "indicative of a possibility not of present actuality" (Dewey 1934, 242). To recognize this in a diagram, as an expression of possibility rather than only an intellectual statement, is to read into its expression its own formative history.

For Alfred Whitehead (1967, 70) such acts of reading themselves constitute a form of perception, a process of "taking account." Taking account here means responding to an event or object and how it "[inflects] the arc of its becoming as a function of its feeling the influence of other events" (Massumi 2011, 26). Perceiving, or interpreting, the communicative potential of two-dimensional diagrams, in turn, becomes its own *event* in a series of interpretative actions — what Tom Conley describes as a process of "stratigraphy" (Conley 2011) (discussed below under "Stratigraphy").

The architect of a diagram is also an archivist. "Taking account" of the formative histories of images and representations is a monumental task. Gilles Deleuze articulates two principles in the work of the archivist: formalization, isolating what is "overstated" in a statement or event, and interpretation, focusing on what is "unsaid" (Deleuze 1988, 15). This frames archiving as a process of recording and assembling phenomena shaped by methodological choices regarding how to register words, phrases, propositions, and other "inscriptions" — where the archive becomes a "discursive formation" and thus a "monument, not a document" (Deleuze 1988, 16). In diagrams, we see a similar process of discursive selection of phenomena: the selective re/presentation of generalized individuals, the relations between them, and relations between influential social forces. Documenting observations and encounters forms the basis of the image. Upon this base are superimposed constructed layers of reference to and inference from previous anthropological works, many of which are themselves assembled archives of personal experience and theoretical influence. More layers, more interpretation. More strata, more stratigraphy.

Diagrams for Charles Peirce (1931), even those developed within tightly structured forms such as blueprints and architectural drawings, are creative endeavors that exhibit affinities on the part of their creators. Diagrams are thus neither entirely fictional nor a presentation of complete fact as much as they are displays of certain individual and disciplinary trajectories. Diagrams thus occupy a position between factuality and fabrication. This echoes the position of a regular map: somewhere between the extremes of being an "adequate imitation" or a "transparent reflection" of an actual territory somewhere, never a "mirror of nature" and more of an instrument with which to shape our perception of the world around us (Bosteels 1998, 147). With diagrams, however, those affinities connect to particular actions, interactions, and processes of fieldwork. Maps remove those traces and connections. Drawing on de Certeau (1984, 120–21) to emphasize how cartographic practices evolved to remove all "traces of the practices" that generate maps, Tim Ingold (2007, 24) argues that maps no longer "bear testimony" to the process of their creation, having "bracketed out the journeys of travellers and the knowledge they brought back" to then create the "impression that the structure of the map springs directly from the structure of the world." Diagrammatic and cartographic practices converge and diverge in multiple ways. The emphasis here is on how diagrams in anthropology *maintain* traces of their own formative histories.

In line with "the rise of modern scientific discourse," the map became a figure disengaged from the bodily, intersubjective experiences and movements that constitute its conditions of possibility (Ingold 2000, 234). The result is a spatial representation assembled from information gathered elsewhere and by other people, information thus alienated from "the particular circumstances of its collection" (Ingold 2000, 234). A critical difference, then, between maps and diagrams is that the latter tend to be incomplete without an accompanying explanation of the characters they contain — be they breathing, spiritual, imaginary, or archetypal characters or beings. Any accompanying text further indicates what are some of the more vital elements of their living arrangements. The information and ideas that generate diagrams in anthropology and frame their delivery are usually not so systematically divorced from the "particular circumstances" of their collection, as in cartography (Ingold 2000, 234). Instead, those circumstances, and the impressions they inscribe within a participating observer, become part of the image itself. Diagrams in anthropology are not only the product of the practices and interactions that led to their creation. Diagrams are also an introduction to those practices and interactions.

Flows, traces, and routes not yet explored: diagrams in anthropology offer us new ways to move through and engage with ongoing histories of exploration, co-creation, and interpretation. This is not unique to anthropology, but it is worth dwelling on how anthropology extends diagrammatic thought in important ways. At the broadest level, the similarities are clear — particularly with reference to movement: A diagram "works as a drawing, a process, a procedure, a temporary moment in between; not the shape of a thing but the outline of a process (of thinking). Hence, dia-grammes should be always seen as moving forms, whether or not they are static" (Ó Maoilearca 2006, 157). While some anthropologists have experimented with animated diagrams that are decidedly not static — see, for example Thorkelson (2016) — my focus is on diagrams of the more typical, two-dimensional, non-animated kind, used as a visual device or product presented in a final form to an audience or readership. As Gell (1999, 11) notes, these static images, these "moments in between," reflect and contribute to "the diagrammatic method" of everyday cognition: non-propositional information about social and ecological environments caught in and interpreted through a perpetually shifting and accumulating series of images. Even in the abstract, to outline a process of thinking, the lines of a diagram tend to imply movement — through relation, connection, correspondence, or direction.

In the shadow of cognition comes interpretation. Historians note how diagrammatic annotations — diagrams in the margins — both served as aids for the producer's cognitive processing *and* as a guide for future readers (Even-Ezra 2021). Félix Guattari's diagrams are also, for example, interpreted to be generative, outlining an "affirmative ontology oriented toward the future, replacing lack (Lacan) and negation (Hegel) with the virtual and the possible [...] diagrams do not represent thought; rather, they generate thought" (Watson 2009, 12). Diagrams are thus also part of the process of making research relations and analytical choices explicit: A diagram

> offers a series of choices and constraints, a roadmap of choices for navigating through data. [...] A drawn diagram offers a narrative argument. [...] Lines and arrows display a functional relation between terms: this path can be followed in this way. [...] The diagram is neither a direct representation of the natural world nor a natural data set, but a suggested theoretical walk through the landscape of data (Osborn 2005, 16).

An outline to generate thought. Define the space, fill the gaps, connect the planes of meaning and intent. Diagrams as anthropological tools: a "graphic shorthand" or "ideogram" loaded with values and meanings both intended and unintended, able to "express relationships of formation and their processes" (Eisenman 2010, 94). Diagrams as "instruments in operation" and as "tools against typologies" (Berkel and Bos 1998, 21). Fielding both the actual and the potential. Sharing histories of investigation as well as projects as yet unfulfilled: the orchestration of information beyond the goals of sense-making.

Diagramming, like sketching or drawing, offers an agile, "graphical language" that operates in the spaces "between notetaking, representation, and abstraction" (Gan 2021, 106–7). This is not to conflate the processes of drawing, sketching, and constructing diagrams, only to point to their shared potential for reinvigorating ethnographic exploration — as ways of seeing, of slowing down, of tracing, and of developing the observations that guide anthropological practice (Colloredo-Mansfeld 2011). Writing about drawing as a mode of analysis, Rachel Douglas-

Jones (2021, 105) describes the effects of using a blank page to help "spatialize and organize your thoughts" and to "think about affinities, shapes, circles, proximities." With this approach, drawing connects a researcher with "the capacity of images to bring forward and assist ethnographic analysis" and with the generative modes of thinking opened up by regularly "shifting medium" from text to image (Douglas-Jones 2021, 94). Building on Bob Simpson's call for humility in ethnographic research away from common "assumptions of control, prediction, surveillance and omnipresence" (Simpson 2006, 135), Douglas-Jones elaborates:

> Ours is not the business of reporting found facts. As we make our fields, they make us, tuning our interests, speaking to our curiosities and concerns [...]. Immersing ourselves in the things we learn to see, whether in the field or at our desk, brings us ethnographic knots and problems, puzzles and jigsaws. (Douglas-Jones 2021, 94)

Outlining, spatializing. These are also the dynamics of re-immersing ourselves in what it takes to imagine, and to create, context-specific diagrams.

Disciplinary archives reveal century-old examples of anthropological practice exploring sketches and drawings as heuristic techniques — visual mediations and strategies for learning *how to see* and for reflecting, and reflecting on, a fieldworker's own subjectivity (Geismar 2014).

The fieldwork sketches in question were made in Vanuatu in 1926–27 by Arthur Bernard Deacon, eventually edited into a 1934 article for *The Journal of the Royal Anthropological Institute* by Camilla Wedgwood — documenting the "Geometrical Drawings from Malekula and Other Islands of the New Hebrides" that include those reproduced here (fig. 4.2). Some of these drawings were recreated from photographs that Deacon took during fieldwork. Many are replications of Deacon's own sketches. But participants or interlocutors in those research processes are the originators of these images — drawings that thus

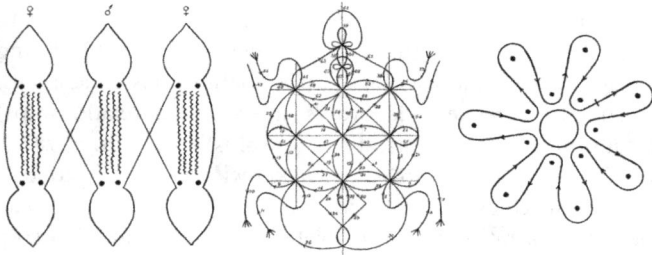

Fig. 4.2. Geometrical drawings ,"Three Ghosts," "Adultery," and "Drop of Water" (Deacon & Wedgwood 1934, 163, 161, 170).

recreate particular performances. Knut Rio (2005, 411) argues that visual recreations extend beyond the capacities of text to hint at the significances of those performances and the diverse forms of knowledge about peoples, places, and possibility that they reflect. At another interpretive level, these moments of ethnographic overlay across text and visual media highlight how research relations, practices, and practitioners can be made visible in new ways. These implications, in turn, impact upon and shape the ways in which ethnographic texts narrativize the processes of their construction, drawing attention to the temporalities and relationalities of knowledge-claims.

Both Object and Means

Social anthropology is relationship-building. The forms of knowledge presented by both visual and textual creations can be described as relational in a double sense: (a) concerning relations between people, or between people and objects, and (b) emerging in dialogue and interaction with diverse others in multiple communities, including people met amidst the friendships and hardships of fieldwork as well as those who constitute institutional networks (Hastrup 2004, 456). In overlapping ways, we encounter the idea that relations are both the object and the means of anthropological inquiry. Anthropological perception: we not only perceive relations between things and people, we also perceive "things as relations" (Strathern 2005, 73). Thus "the relation" is anthropology's "heuristic and object" and also its "field": "anthropologists use relationships (made with informants) to relate social orders (interpersonal relationships) to cultural logics (categorical relationships)" (Kelly 2012, 78). It is in this sense that anthropological knowledge is understood to be a "social achievement" (Crick 1982, 20), as a relational, social phenomenon rather than an isolated, individual one (Hastrup 2004, 456). Relationship-building is a knowledge-making process.

Relationality precedes reality. Whatever exists of the latter we come to know through the former. Our representations of these processes are guides *to* them and *through* them rather than totalizing constructions or depictions *of* them. Following this thread, our understanding of how these processes unfold is mediated by the representations of thought, of action, and of time passing that are made available to us and created, consumed, and interpreted by us. Representations guide interpretation rather than determine it (Fabian 1990, 754). Johannes Fabian argues that representation in anthropology is better thought of as "praxis" within which individual texts and images can be considered as "acts" or "performances" that are "convincing," primarily according to their ability to communicate and persuade rather than to prove (Fabian 1990, 756–57). Any such performances are always in danger of excluding or minimizing the contribution and historical agency of the people whose lives they represent. Those deeper forms of collaboration remain relatively rare within the academy. Nonetheless, the notion of representation as praxis refocuses how diagrams can be interpreted and read — not as tools of representation, assessed with reference to a quantifiable degree of accuracy in replicating an independently-existing reality or terrain, but as visual devices that support processes of knowledge creation, communication, and dissemination by contributing to the wider epistemic fields that give shape to those processes. The classical referents of anthropology — including diagrams — are only classical till their significance is radically reimagined, rejected, or reassessed:

With the acknowledgement of knowledge as relational, both historical events and social experience have lost their immediate status as positive evidence of the connections between events, actions and experiences. […] Anthropological knowledge, then, is not simply knowledge about particular events, practices and ideas, but about the processes by which these come to appear meaningful. (Hastrup 2004, 468)

As a construction (an assemblage of observational material), a diagram functions as a tool that extends observation, enabling us to "see the connections" that link relations of similarity and difference across different aspects of daily life and existence by giving those relations visual form (Bourdieu 1990, 10). It is precisely the act of "cumulating and juxtaposing" relations of opposition and equivalence that creates the density of diagrams: offering a view of synchronized material that can be (re)viewed in an instant, revealing relationships, as well as contradictions, that might not be observable in the usual temporal flow of experience (Bourdieu 1990, 82). Interpretation renewed. Previously unnoticed overlaps and affinities, brought to light (Bourdieu 1990, 82). Analytical, interpretive flaws and discontinuities exposed. Reading diagrams through these acts of observation and interpretation, then, is something that author and audience alike embark upon, the one to reflect on the limitations of their own knowledge-creating practices, the other to be introduced to practices and ideas as part of broader analytical, comparative projects.

These interpretive processes of totalization and synchronization have epistemic effects. What benefits are to be gained from the potential for immediate, coherent transmission of information through diagrammatic images? And what falsities are created by interpreting relations between elements of a visual model as factual encounters observable between people and things? For Bourdieu, diagrams most effectively operate in a productive space between two characterized poles of representational praxis, as works that are "less logical than structuralist pan-logicism would have it and more logical then the inchoate, uncertain evocation of intuitionism would suggest" (Bourdieu 1990, 210). It is in that space that diagrams as models can be generative — revealing new connections in both the analysis and interpretation of social life. This generative tension is key to understanding diagrams in anthropology. The immediacy of seeing complements the "sequentiality" of auditory and tactile impressions: "when our eyes are presented with things that are next to each other, we gain an overview; we can compare different sorts of things to see similarities and differences, as well as recognize relationships, proportions and patterns within the vast diversity. Diagrams make the dissimilar comparable" (Krämer 2010, 29). While the atemporality critique in anthropology addresses what is missing from diagrams — the messy emergence of relational everyday life and the politics of mutuality across power asymmetries — diagrams as knowledge devices have the potential to show us what we are missing in our own analyses, revealing new connections that might otherwise have escaped our perception within the constant flow of relationality and intersubjectivity.

Diagrams to Discomfort

The anthropological diagram is not the abstract diagram. The abstract diagram is never drawn. The abstract diagram is the presentation of relations between forces and the "distribution of the power to affect and the power to be affected" within a particular social field (Deleuze 1988, 72). The abstract diagram is "an architectonic mapping of the play of forces, one that is easily transposable to other domains and capable of being actualized in different ways" (Bialecki 2016, 716). The abstract diagram is different from how we might understand *structure* due to the diagram being unstable and diffuse, revealing "unexpected affinities" and only ever mapping intensities and potentialities rather than fixed points that might be used to predict the effects of actions (Deleuze 1988, 36). Such a diagram never "functions in order to represent a persisting world" but instead, by expressing the potential and emergence of relations between forces, "produces a new kind of reality"; it is thus "neither the subject of history" nor an attempt to "survey" history (Deleuze 1988, 36). There can be the abstract diagram of sovereignty, of discipline, a Greek or Roman diagram, a feudal diagram (Deleuze 1988, 40, 85), or the Napoleonic diagram, evolving between modes of hierarchy and control (Deleuze 1988, 35). The abstract diagram helps us think beyond structure and to think through the nature of the abstract itself:

> What the diagram diagrams is a dynamic interrelation of relations. [...] The diagram is false, in that it contracts a multiplicity of levels and matters into its own homogeneous substance. But it is true, in that it envelops in that substance the same affect, and because it reproduces the in-betweenness of the affect in the fracturing of its own genesis. The expression of meaning is true in its falseness to itself, and false in its trueness to its content. (Massumi 1992, 16)

The abstract diagram is a "becoming of forces" or a "map of becoming" (Conley 2011, 166). It is a construct that seeks to pattern these emergent relations; a model that gives shape to relations that are perpetually the subject of change; an interrogation that emerges through manifold "points of emergence or creativity, unexpected conjunctions or improbable continuums" (Deleuze 1988, 35). Every diagram is "intersocial" and "constantly evolving" since a diagram "never functions in order to represent a persisting world but produces a new kind of reality, a new model of truth" (Deleuze 1988, 35). Here, the emphasis is on the possibility of forces and forms of interaction being made actual, since the diagram is itself an abstract dimension of "virtuality" that maps "possibilities before they are actualized" (Zdebik 2012, 7). An anthropological diagram is not an abstract diagram in these Deleuzian terms, but the latter draws attention to the underlying focus of the current work: the interplay of possibilities, potentialities, and contingencies.

There is a risk of blurring distinctions here. Raising the concept of the Deleuzian, abstract diagram in the context of a discussion of actual, drawn diagrams might only cause confusion. These are such different worlds, different concepts. But they are bridged, in part, through reconfigurations of what we understand as diagrammatic thinking and practice. With reference to the work of artists, specifically painters, Deleuze traces the process of reducing or resolving the infinite possibilities of a blank canvas to or within a finalized form and image: "They say that the painter is already in the canvas, where he or she encounters all the figurative and probabilistic givens that occupy and preoccupy the canvas" (Deleuze 2003, 99). Sher Doruff similarly describes the "bridge" as a multiple space where deriving the actual from the possible, the concrete from the abstract, forms part of a deliberate intervention in the flow of experience: "There are co-extensive registers of relation present between diagramming as an abstract machine and as a formalizing realization of that abstraction — those sketches, drawings and mappings making their way to form, to the desired construction of the aggregate, the more or less concrete assemblage" (Doruff 2009, 123). A preoccupation with what might have been, with how things might have been otherwise. An anthropological cornerstone.

Other conceptual links between the abstract diagram and actual diagrams emerge when we interpret the word "diagram" in each context as being a "technique of existence" (Massumi 1998, 47). That is, understanding the diagram as a way of processing change over time; a procedure for navigating the "complexity of experience's passing"; a technique of interpreting those critical moments where "one moment of experience's passing passes into another, informing it of (in-forming it with) the potential to become again" (Massumi 2011, 25). Reading a diagram as a technique of existence means tracing the processes through which the "unstable forces of a social field" differentially affect how "art and life are performed and lived" and whereby "the power relations between these forces charge and guide the individuating subject amidst the multiple contingencies of acting otherwise" (Doruff 2009, 121). The otherwise is always an inversion — for example, of the done, the completed, the documented, the experienced, or the "wise."

To act otherwise is not merely individual behavior change that makes minor modifications to established roles within systems of violence, as if selecting different products for purchase within the apocalypse of limitless consumer choice. Acting otherwise is submitting to the challenge of decentering oneself; pursuing an inversion of the immediate and the familiar. Undermining how we know what we think we know in order to expand the terms and terminology of knowledge creation. This is another anthropological cornerstone. Diagrams are tools for the always-preliminary task: to confront power and to discomfort ourselves. Those deceptively simple-sounding goals.

An individually drawn diagram, then, can reflect or reveal different connections and configurations of the social — actual, past, and potential — beyond those that it directly recreates or describes. Diagrams, in this sense, are both microcosm and model of the anthropological project: "the point of anthropology is not to tell the world *as it is* (which would be practically impossible) but to interpret it and to suggest possible (theoretical) connections within it" (Hastrup 2004, 468, emphasis in original). Revealing unexpected affinities. Charting a dynamic interrelation of relations. Reading diagrams in these ways reframes the drawn diagram itself is an invitation to reassess social possibilities, potentialities, and contingencies:

Diagrams are simple drawings or figures that we think with or think through. The idea of thinking through a diagram is crucial not only because a diagram provides order and stability but because it is a vehicle for destabilization and discovery. [...A]ny figure that is drawn is accompanied by an expectancy that it will be redrawn. [...W]hile a diagram may have been used visually to reinforce an idea one moment, the next it may provide a means of seeing something never seen before. (Knoespel 2001, 146–47)

Stratigraphy

Sahlins's model of modes of exchange (1972) considers all non-market exchanges and transactions as reflections of different kinds of *reciprocity* and proposes a correlation between modes of economic transaction and modes of social organization, such as the house, lineage, village, or community (Widlok 2013, 15).

In diagrammatic form (fig. 4.3), Sahlins maps modes of transaction with the living arrangements of those involved: the result is a "single two-dimensional graph of concentric circles with house and generalized reciprocity at its center, negative reciprocity at the outside and balanced reciprocity in between" (Widlok 2013, 15). In examining this diagram in more detail, we have three areas of focus: (a) the relationships between this diagram and previous work, that is, the degree to which it synthesizes others' ideas and contributions; (b) its role and influence in subsequent debates; and (c) the design and import of its immediate features.

Describing this diagram as a graph reflects its content and expression: an intersection of x and y axes in turn suggesting a relation of correspondence (if not proportionality) between reciprocity, kinship, and residential sectors. No exact coordinates are specified for any one type of transaction. As Sahlins notes, it is a "general model." This means our interpretation of how and why two points could meet — within one of the many shaded dots read to connote possible moments of interaction and exchange — is always approximate, informed by contextual detail supplied elsewhere, outside of and separate from the diagram itself. Neither the lines nor shading depict or represent known individuals or visible objects. The graphisms deployed could not be described as "distorted, inaccurate or illusory" since criteria of "accuracy, precision or realism" do not apply in the context of such an open-ended, interpretive model (Lynch 1991, 10). Subsequent disciplinary disputes regarding "accuracy" have been directed at Sahlins's overall model rather than targeting specific faults or issues with this diagram *of* the model. In part, this is due to the arrangement of the diagram as a two-

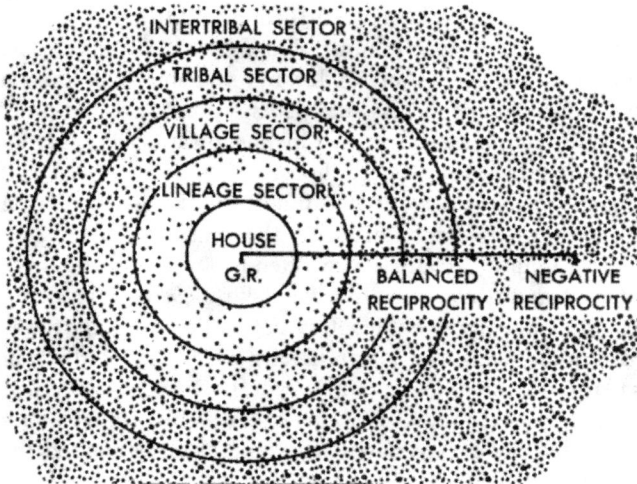

Fig. 4.3. "Reciprocity and Kinship Residential Sectors" (Sahlins 1972, 199).

dimensional image rather than, more straightforwardly, as a graph plotting two related variables on a pair of axes at right angles. Compared to a regular graph, a diagram invites and enables more numerous interpretations, applications, and comparisons.

A number of diagrammatic features enable these comparisons and explorations. The dots are nonuniform in size and orientation, suggesting variance across degrees of shading within the diagram and across points of exchange in the model. Aside from being removed from areas surrounding text included in the diagram (to render said text more distinct and legible), the array of dots is irregular. They are not entirely un-patterned, however. They are clearly arranged with reduced intensity toward the center (nearer the "house"), an effect that serves to distinguish between radial zones ("sectors") and also highlights the central area, emphasizing this "house" as the location of most frequent exchange interactions. The radiality of concentric circles further emphasizes a sense of difference between the house and other sectors. A shift in scale between them also introduces the idea of movement, out along innumerable radii that converge upon a common center. Such routes reflect innumerable potential journeys, imagined encounters, and paths — points on, and trajectories through, the diagram that incline toward each other and meet at the shared root of the "house."

Each "sector" interrupts the trajectory of movement from, and sense of difference between, the central house and the "intercommunity" realm which extends out beyond the frame of the diagram into unbounded outskirts (Sahlins 1972, 219). This indefinite domain denotes the purlieus of this model: surrounding areas that are indirectly connected to the more regularly occupied, more central spaces. Outlying but visited; adjacent; not unknown. The circles that denote inner sectors are regular but the overlay of dots and shading suggest they are approximate: they do not have to be seen as evenly-spaced circles nor do their perimeters need to be regular. The borders between them are fuzzy and imprecise, subject to contextual variation. Imprecision entering the image also as a result of the production methods available at the time of publication. This is a simple model which "represents some features of reality better than others" and reflects a core argument of the work within which it is found, a work that has subsequently become a focus of theoretical and semantic debate: the idea that "very close and very distant relationships" are not necessarily associated with transfers and exchange of "balanced reciprocity" (Widlok 2013, 15). Any notion of reality becomes known through actual and potential relationships. Sahlins's diagram is a theoretical provocation: a map of possibilities.

At the time, Sahlins was explicit in his intention to create a "general model" in part by drawing on work conducted at other times and in other contexts — works that also addressed the relationship between reciprocity and social interaction. Within such a generalized account, he calls for attention to how the varying "power of community" is witnessed in its effects, particularly with regard to how distance and space are delineated (Sahlins 1972, 197). Such broad terms and abstractions would struggle to hold any weight, or to be relatable to other contexts, were they not themselves built upon specific instances and drawn from particular prior examples. In these readings, there is a shift in what the diagram is seen to be modelling — focusing less on the decontextualized representation of social life and interaction and more on the diagram as a model for thought. One of the enduring inferences of this model is that exchange relations are shaped in terms of "the moral expectations involved" (Widlok 2013, 15), for example, in the case of a commodity trader whose happiness results from having received a "more valued item for a less valued one" from a distant customer (Gell 1999, 85). Here, the diagram, or rather readings of and responses to the diagram, reflect concerns that fueled the discipline at the time when the diagram was created and discussed. Possibilities are reduced to *types*. Assumptions are made about the yet-to-be-actualized.

Any discipline exists through a shared set of assumptions. Drawing directly on Raymond Firth (1951, 144), who concluded from his work exploring Siuai exchange relations that "economic relations rest on moral foundations," Sahlins specifically embedded "morality" as a third term in the model alongside "sectoral division" and "reciprocity variation" (Sahlins 1972, 198). Similarly, with direct reference to Clyde Kluckhohn's (1949, 366) work on Navajo philosophy, we are presented with another approach to the intersection of morality with these two terms. Contextual, rather than absolute, morality means that each situation determines what might be considered acceptable behavior: deception in exchange relations, for example, might be morally accepted when trading with competitors, distant others, or friends of enemies (Sahlins 1972, 200). Further reference is made to Douglas Oliver's work (1955, 454–55), also addressing Siuai exchange relations, and the use of "hard bargaining and deceit" only within certain distant social sectors — specifically in order to "make as much profit as possible from such transactions" (Sahlins 1972, 197). Taken together, these sources combine to make the diagram an abstract amalgam of interactions and reciprocal exchanges that are both actual and potential — a combination that is only realized in conjunction with the accompanying text.

The result is a model of the anthropological project that, like the Deleuzian diagram, "maps possibilities" and invites further reassessment of the social forces that affect how life is lived and how life might be lived.

To read an image, to read a diagram, as we would read a cohesive text is also to perform the quasi-archaeological work of uncovering the conditions of their creation (Davies and Parrinder 2004). Reading the visible fragments involves deciphering disciplinary tropes, trends, commitments, and those unifying assumptions. Much of this content is *found,* even if it has not been placed there to be found. With this approach, the Sahlins diagram contains layers of information derived from (and built upon) previous works. This layering of ideas is akin to Deleuzian *strata:* "historical formations, positivities or empiricities[, ...] 'sedimentary beds' [made] from things and words, from seeing and speaking, from the visible and the sayable, from bands of visibility and fields of readability, from contents and expressions" (Deleuze 1988, 47). Sahlins's general model is less a record of these prior investigations and more of an abbreviation of some of their critical observations and underlying implications. In this sense, the general model is not just an attempt to present information in a way that facilitates comparison with other social contexts. It becomes a model for thought, the historical strata that can be unearthed serving to challenge or extend theoretical frameworks. The diagrammatic framing of concepts thus enables comparative anthropologies by highlighting "recurrent self-reflexive functional patterns" while also "allowing a space for variance in the creation of concrete assemblies of discourse and practice, as well as for different relative speeds and intensities through which these forces act on one another" (Bialecki 2016, 716–17). Further possibilities emerge within each trace of their origins.

The tensions are always there: outdated ideas, off-putting terminology, the sense that any such model cannot escape its latent power to become a model for control, to perform a role in constituting logics of domination. Still, expanding on these conclusions, rereading diagrams in anthropology favors an approach that does not privilege individual narratives but instead fore-grounds how different works mobilize political, aesthetic, and philosophical problems (Manning 2019, 363). This is the spirit of an 'inverse museum,' where what is elevated is not the collection itself but people's reactions to it. Those reactions include how we live and work with, against, and in spite of, canonical relics and their ongoing presence as real ghosts bearing the will of their creators. These reactions become processes of de-individualization, of un-disciplining. That is, by reading diagrams in ways that refuse their assumed neutrality, that refuse the assumed authority of social theories and aesthetics upheld by the author(s) and their scholarly communities, and that instead seek to 'read' the ethical and political flaws within certain visual methods as further impetus for redirecting current practice toward more mutual ends.

Deciphering those shifting Deleuzian *strata* exposes further similarities and resemblances between an anthropological diagram and a Deleuzian diagram. The latter is less like a map and more like "several superimposed maps" — a store of overlapping points of "creativity, change, and resistance" (Deleuze 1988, 44). Those points are both conceptual and actual. Gathering these multiple points together in condensed form, in a singular image, the diagram enables dialogue across a succession of diagrams or, in the context of anthropology, across different research projects and fieldwork contexts. Comparison, here, is *stratigraphy:* a process in which a reader deciphers each theoretical or historical stratum within a layering of "superimposed maps" and ideas (Conley 2011, 166). Stratigraphy involves disentangling and comparing (and disentangling-in-order-to-compare) multiple contributions of distinct, precursor works and the influence of multiple historical moments. Stratigraphy also includes the work required to identify and describe strata, since strata do not occur in some neat, bounded, or "pure" form — more typically we are confronted with blurred or hybrid forms (De Landa 1998). Re-reading diagrams in anthropology is another form of such stratigraphic work. By generating an "overview effect" — an immediate, simultaneous perspective on an unfinished realm of proposed, actual, and potential relations — diagrams as visual schematics become "translatable and mobile" and therefore "amenable to transmission and reproduction, circulation and translation" (Carver 2023, 21865). With each act of comparison or translation, stratigraphic practices further multiply and interact.

As noted above in "Potentiality, Surplus, and Possibilities Not Yet Explored," diagrams are amalgamations: the selective (re)presentation of real or generalized individuals or communities, and the graphic plotting of social forces and interrelations that connect and constitute these characters and their different sociocultural contexts. Each subsequent, superimposed layer is constructed out of what Deleuze calls "inscriptions": references to and interpretations of other anthropological texts or images, each of which is itself inscribed with the influence of specific fieldwork experiences and theoretical debates. Comparison is connection. Each diagram becomes a multiple space, or pivot point, where movement is stilled and where potentiality is exhibited.

Deciphering historical strata, mapping potentialities amidst the play of forces in a given social field, and plotting the emergence of relations amidst the superimposition of layers of abstract maps — these are interpretive and analytical steps a long way from the typical disciplinary focus, such as on the inversion of tree metaphors in kinship diagrams or questions around the use of diagrams as evidence. Still, the Sahlins graph illustrates how a reductive and apparently simple diagram is also deeply implicated within these broader historical processes of contestation and knowledge-creation.

Any appearance of diagrammatic simplicity is, itself, misleading — not least because not all lines are created equal. There are violin strings, the veins of a leaf, lines "made by walking," threads and traces, ruptures, cuts, cracks, and creases (Ingold 2007). There is the endless line of the horizon, a permanent presence but transient target, always shifting and plural, encircling everything for everyone and multiplied by the countless number of perspectives from where it can be seen. Lines connect, lines deceive. Reading diagrams is impossible without grappling with the many lives of lines.

Lines, Rhizomes, Guidance

Lines create space. The "simple, sober line," following Michel Foucault, performs an instrumental role in classifying knowledge, filtering out "excessive elements" from reality and translating the "vital elements" into a form within the "flat surface of the page" (Zdebik 2012, 66). Lines can be arranged through "labels, geometric boundaries, vectors, and symmetries" that are often used to "convey a sense of orderly flows of causal influences, discrete factors [or known relations] in a tightly contained, homogenous field" (Lynch 1991, 12). Lines are intentional or, at least, suggest and betray the intentions of an actor somewhere at a certain point in time. But even apparently fixed lines cannot escape their relation with the potentiality which that fixity implies:

> The line already marks a space; it marks it out by dividing and creating space. And yet, a line neither draws nor plots out of necessity. The diagram need neither present nor hold to the spatial possibilities of something other than itself. Nor, for that matter, do lines and diagrams exist as ends in themselves. There may be a possibility other than that demanded by the literal. (Benjamin 1998, 36)

The possibilities are endless, often inscrutable. Lines are also relations. Similarly limitless. Citing James Gibson (1986), Brian Massumi details the diagrammatic line as both a boundary or edge (an inverse relation) and as an invitation to reconnect spaces that transcend and exist between edges (a renewed relation): "Draw a line on a piece of paper. The line repeats the edge. The line repeats the relating. 'The line is the relating; see it and you see relation; feel it and you feel the relation'" (Massumi 1998, 45). In anthropological attempts to diagram the lives of others, lines are not only relational; lines are political inscriptions.

They are at it again. Deleuze and Guattari develop two contrasting kinds of line. The first kind of line is "subordinated to the point" and "the space it constitutes is one of striation. [...] Lines of this type [form a] binary, arborescent system" (Deleuze and Guattari 1987, 505). Lines like this "represent the classical tree, the arborescent system" in direct contrast to a second type of line which is "akin to the rhizome model" (Zdebik 2012, 75). Rhizomatic lines are not bound to fixed points and contours but instead pass across and between multiple spaces and connections (Deleuze and Guattari 1987, 505). Arborescent lines. Rhizomatic lines. Different uses, different ethical implications. In Part III, "The Framework Sets the Limits / The Limits Are the Framework," we saw how inverted family trees began to grow their roots at the top, the tree itself a linear model of descent, written in code (Bouquet 1995; Ingold 2000). This is not merely a matter of appearances. Images are chains of influence and affect.

The tree has been widely used as a "potent image" in Western intellectual history — in diagrammatical form to represent both "hierarchies of control and schemes of taxonomic division" and also, and above all, "chains of genealogical connection" (Ingold 2000, 134). The rhizome model, by contrast, looks beyond the "static and linear, arborescent and dendritic imagery of the genealogical model" to focus on worlds in movement and the living beings, lands, and relationships that constitute and embrace those worlds (Ingold 2000, 140). Rhizomatic lines create worlds where "every part or region enfolds, in its growth, its relations with all the others. [...] a continually ravelling and unravelling relational manifold" (Ingold 2000, 140). The implications for thinking otherwise, for reconsidering connection and relationality, for rethinking boundaries and a/symmetries, are not limited to theoretical moves. The rhizome model offers guidance for interpreting diverse relational models.

In her description of Yarralin worldviews, Deborah Bird Rose describes individuals as shaped by their own personal "angle of perception" which itself reflects shifting combinations of the influence of matrilineal identities and diverse relationships that tie people "into other species and to the workings of the world" (Rose 2000, 221). The diagram drawn to reflect this resembles Deleuze and Guattari's rhizome: it is "a dense and tangled cluster of interlaced threads or filaments, [in which] any point [can] be connected to any other" (Ingold 2000, 140). Rhizomatic lines place us always amid multiple spaces, traces, and connections. This is an orientation that moves us away — politically, ethically, conceptually — from the dominance of binaries and linearity. From that move we can derive an openness to as yet-unrealized or unnoticed affinities.

Rose's description of relationships and contexts — based on Yarralin ideas about wisdom, difference, and interconnection — includes the influence of physical and relational positioning on perception (fig. 4.4):

> An angle of perception is a boundary, and boundaries are both necessary and arbitrary. Necessity lies in the fact that there are no relationships unless there are parts, and without relationships there is only uniformity and chaos. Arbitrariness lies in the fact that since all parts are ultimately interconnected, the particular boundary drawn at a given point is only one of many possible boundaries. Each line in [Figure 24] is both a boundary and a relationship. Each node (A, B, C, etc.) is both a context and an angle of vision, another centre. [...] One particular human angle defines our world as it is because it is we who are looking. Perception distorts, but wisdom lies in knowing that distortion is not understanding. (Rose 2000, 222)

Perception is positioning. An unfinished act, an evolving process. Relationality is precursive to understanding.

Studying how both physical and relational positioning influences perception reflects a number of key points addressed in the paragraphs above: that our understanding of the anthropological project and of the anthropological object is emergent; that processes of knowledge-creation are relational (Hastrup 2004); that those processes are dependent on the stories peo-

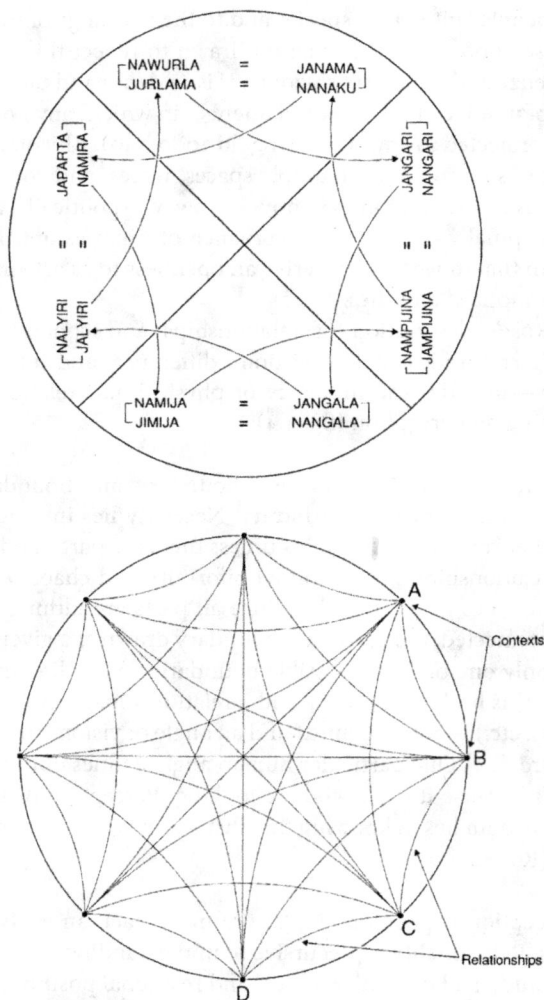

Fig. 4.4. Top: "Figure 9 – Sixteen subsection categories showing circles of women, brothers, and marriage partners" (Rose 2000, 77). Bottom: "Figure 24 – Relationships and Contexts" (Rose 2000, 222).

ple use to make sense of their own actions (Barnes 1967); and that subsequent routes to interpretation of those knowledge-constructions are implicated in diverse social histories and locations — enabling multiple readings of any one image or text (Bourdieu 1990). These final examples also illustrate how diagrams can act as guides, shaping the narratives that surround both their formation and their interpretation (Osborn 2005, 16). The translation Rose performs from specific coordinates and named individuals — Yarralin marriage practices — to abstract ideas and perspectives — relationships and contexts — reflects this quality of guidance and indication to be found and potentially explored further in anthropological diagrams.

This recalls the different kinds of model that diagrams can function as and become, as described in Part III, "Diagrams as Stories, Diagrams as Models." Diagrams are not blueprints. Blueprints are technical drawings that resemble Clifford Geertz's "model *for*" — providing a basis for action and organizing intervention in physical relationships. A blueprint is also a drawing with a particular purpose: to "depict an object in such a particular way that the person who follows the line of the drawing will be able to build [or recreate] it" (Zdebik 2012, 74). In contrast, diagrams invite other responses, other readings of the line. In Rose's relationships diagram, "following the line" provides us with different perspectives on the formation and perpetuation of social relations and, crucially, guides the expectations people place on each other due to the weight of their connections. These are diagrams that "provide a possible outline or itinerary, but do not determine the specifics of how a journey will unfold" (Osborn 2005, 16). These are diagrams that translate ethnographic detail into illuminating theoretical images. These are images that might *bring to light* new connections and observations. Synthesized materials, accessible in a visual form, enable analysts and readers alike to discern relations between people and objects that might have previously remained elusive. Diagrams here become guides along suggested, indicated, or as-yet-undefined paths.

The range of diagrams across the anthropological canon can be read, together or individually, as a snapshot of the discipline's own fraught archive — tracing discursive formations that serve multiple purposes in diverse contexts, though never quite able to escape their particular moments of origin and creation. Monuments, not documents (Deleuze 1988). Through these layered inscriptions, diagrams tell us about epistemic processes within anthropology and across the social sciences; about dominant intellectual trends; and about efforts to question, challenge, confront, and undermine disciplinary understandings of anthropology's own boundaries and potentialities.

V

Burning to Prepare the Ground

Ignite to Expose

Histories of diagrams in anthropology echo histories of anthropology itself: problematic, contested, unfinished.

At times these echoes resonate quite directly, for example, when key debates of the day become solidified in a diagram's outline, content, and expression. Parallel movements, condensed thought. Cutting the form to fit the theory.

At other times, the echoes are almost indistinct. Or rather, the histories are no longer parallel; they are punctuated and circular. We see this in some of the clear, formal similarities between diagrams published in works separated by almost a century. As if the form still fits today, and will fit forever. The mantra that characterized an early, and ongoing, disciplinary commitment to family trees with their roots at the top: an abstraction for all; the abstract of everyone.

That kind of tree is still with us. Other diagrammatic forms also persist, or periodically re-emerge. And so, what is it to continue working — reading, writing, learning, researching — among such canonical ruins? Ruins that do not merely continue to exist (sometimes gathering dust) but which, many of which, continue to influence academic perspectives and practices? This question was our starting point. In response, in defense of these two-dimensional works: they embrace the immediacy of the visual, a cognitive intervention to suggest, reveal, or reinforce connections that might otherwise remain out of view, out of reach.

So much can escape our perception amid the bounteous flow of everyday relationality and intersubjectivity. As argued above, relations are both the object and the means of anthropological inquiry. Diagrams open a door to multiple other ways of visualizing and therefore conceptualizing social relations, including those we will never experience ourselves. That open-ended potential reflects the surplus of everyday life — how the flow of experience exceeds representation, whether textual or visual — which further connects anthropological methods, objects, referents, and knowledge devices. Ideas outside the linearity of text.

This book has also studied what is involved in (re)reading diagrams in anthropology: decoding tropes, expanding contested histories, disentangling thought from form. These are critical tasks, actions, performances. Reading diagrams in these ways reflects what others have identified as a central focus for anthropology as a whole: using processes of inquiry to seek out vital connections and unexpected possibilities.

But, phrased like this, the case for embracing diagrams is broad. If their potential is to be pursued, with care, diagrams could contribute to other moves to expand the anthropological palette. That is, expansion through more meaningful engagement with worlds-of-practice that are sensorial, aesthetic, phenomenological, aural, visual, corporeal, emotional, creative, performative, experimental, or collaborative — the many forms of practice that support liberatory inquiry, imagination, and respectful solidarity. Anthropology "unmoored" from the classics, as Ryan Jobson (2020) has it, is aware of but not beholden to the dicta of overly familiar referents, precursors, objects, and their shadows. Disciplines discipline, but their borders are weak. Even Guillermo Gómez-Peña's "Anthropoloco" figure carries a lens for looking, crossing from side(s) to side(s) often enough to evade the self-appointed guards enforcing boundaries of thought (Gómez-Peña and Rivero de Beer 2009). The inverse of disciplinarity is not multi- or inter- but a-. Decentered work is both a scholarly goal but also, more broadly, a reflection of what is increasingly clear: that the center will no longer hold, nor hold us.

Given all this, why compile a collection of some of anthropology's classical and not-so-classical referents and identifiable tropes, scrutinize them, and hold them up to be gazed upon and, in some small way, to be regarded as curious objects of cultural activity? Is such a compilation not somehow self-defeating? The response here echoes the introduction to this book. The goal remains an embrace of *kairos*-driven research: orienting our work to address immediate, pressing needs and objectives; building less violent, less destructive praxis out of rekindled relationships; refusing dogmatism and disciplinary orthodoxy; asking not only "Where are we now?" but also "How did we get here?" as an orientation for future-facing engagements. With an inverse museum, the collection matters less than reactions to it. But the collection still matters, most likely also in ways that we do not fully anticipate. The collection is the crooked path that got us here, the museum merely a snapshot of some of many different routes taken. The delinearity of diagrams offers another dimension to explore as we look ahead, and as we look around.

Evade. Dissociate. It is one thing to embrace some of the under-explored aesthetic and communicative potentialities of visual devices. It is another project entirely to commit to the potential of the untold. Working with, grappling with, the potential for things to be otherwise — another anthropological cornerstone — gets us so far. What would it be to invert the untold in order to place it at the center of academic practice? An inverse anthropology. Or a "potential history," which Ariella Aïsha Azoulay (2019, 286) describes as "a commitment to attend to the potentialities that the institutional forms of imperial violence — borders, nation-states, museums, archives, and laws — try to make obsolete or turn into precious ruins." Those same institutions are the inverse of the potential; they rigidly insist on familiar orderings of "the past" and they render the archive a "graveyard of political life that insists that time is a linear temporality" (Azoulay 2019, 186). The potential is routinely sidelined, silenced, mis-placed, and de-placed. Abstracted. But even though diagrams are themselves a move of abstraction, a generous reading of diagrams aligns with Anna Grimshaw's (2001) account of Cubist art and similarities between the two: gathering together multiple perspectives, attending to relationships and interactions, and opening up the act of rendering connections visible to redefinition. Here diagrams contain other potentialities: suggesting connections that might otherwise have escaped our perception or analyses. Critical work. And another way to (re)connect the operative world of relational fieldwork with the representative world of everything that follows it.

As stated above, a critical anthropology — rooted in a refusal of canonical hierarchies and occlusions — requires a reorientation of ethics, relationality, and political action beyond figurative acts of burning. Complicity is not so easily denied. But such critical acts of burning may also embody some of the effects of actual flames. That is, the preparation of the ground — our shared ground — for the kinds of work that are relevant, and required, today. This is not to glorify or misunderstand diverse cultures of burning or actual practices of fire management, as frequently happens in ecologist and environmentalist spheres. Instead, such burning means refusing adherence to disciplinary normalcy. Igniting, exposing, and contesting all the barriers we face in reviving collaborative kinds of visual, political, and relational action.

VI

Sources: Image Inventory

This section presents contextual information for the fifty-two images featured in Part II, "Images Gathered (A Fragmented Crowd)" — the collection that forms this inverse museum. For each diagram, the information provided includes publication date, author name (with biographical dates, when available), and the original caption that accompanied the image in its initial presentation. For diagrams not discussed elsewhere in this book, a brief account is provided of the diagram's connection to anthropological debates or the author's stated purpose for each image. This is an image inventory: a catalog, of sorts.[1]

The museum catalog is an instrument of power. Its pages systematize displacement.

Mapping the plunder, piece by piece. Codifying works removed from their original home.

Each decontextualized item is assigned a new, and specific, institutional home. A way to locate the dislocated. Perhaps presented with a glossy finish, or featuring design innovations deployed to boost audience engagement. Keep them coming

---

1 Unless mentioned otherwise, these images are presented under the doctrine of fair use.

back. Every visit is counted. Each record is always ready to be updated.

These words, insufficient, might be all you ever learn about an image.

To complete the picture, what else needs to be known?

Or, counterpoint: incompleteness is a desirable invitation to exploration — a means of reimagination, a perpetual but unfinished end.

What remains is potential. And work against silencing — the work of recentering potentialities and reclaiming a relational impulse for anthropology closer to Mary Oliver's instructions for life itself: "Pay attention. Be astonished. Tell about it" (Oliver 2008, 36). The inverse of the finished: imagining and imaging limitless forms of interconnectedness to be embraced, collectively reworked, and communicated.

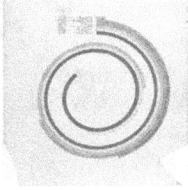

Publication date: 1900.

Author: William Edward Burghardt Du Bois (1868–1963).

Original caption: "Assessed value of household and kitchen furniture owned by Georgia Negroes. Circular bar graph shows value of furniture between 1875 and 1899; Chart prepared by W.E.B. Du Bois for The Exhibit of American Negroes at the Paris Exposition Universelle in 1900 to show the economic and social progress of African Americans since emancipation" (Du Bois 1900a, n.p.).

This image is held by the US Library of Congress (item 2013650445). More chart than diagram, this image has since been repurposed within original artworks by the Color Coded collective (https://colorcoded.la/) — a series of powerful collages combining infographics, figures, and technical drawings from patent applications — as published on the website of Ruha Benjamin (https://www.ruhabenjamin.com/credits).

Image in the public domain.

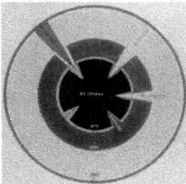

Publication date: 1900.

Author: William Edward Burghardt Du Bois (1868–1963).

Original caption: "Assessed valuation of all taxable property owned by Georgia Negroes. Diagram shows value of taxable property owned by African Americans in Georgia between 1875 and 1890. Chart prepared by Du Bois for the Negro Exhibit of the American Section at the Paris Exposition Universelle in 1900 to show the economic and social progress of African Americans since emancipation" (Du Bois 1900b, n.p.). This figure is also held by the US Library of Congress (item 2013650442). Both of these images by Du Bois use data visualization techniques that pre-date the formal, and explicit, adoption of diagramming techniques within anthropology, as subsequently pursued by William H.R. Rivers and others.

Image in the public domain.

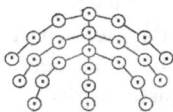

Publication date: 1871.

Author: Lewis Henry Morgan (1818–1881).

Original caption: "In the 'Ancient Laws and Institutes of Wales [1841],' there is a curious diagram illustrative of the Welsh system of consanguinity, of which [this] is a copy. (*Vide* British Records, Commission Series, Ancient Laws and Institutes of Wales, book xi, cf. iv, p. 605)" (Morgan 1871, 46).

Morgan's diagrams are discussed in Part III, "Inversions, Continued."

Image in the public domain.

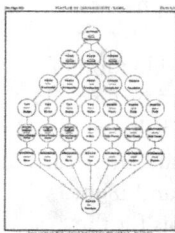

Publication date: 1871.

Author: Lewis Henry Morgan (1818–1881).

Original caption: "Diagram of Consanguinity: Tamil" (Morgan 1871, 594 / Plate XIV).

Morgan's diagrams are discussed in Part III, "Inversions, Continued."

Image in the public domain.

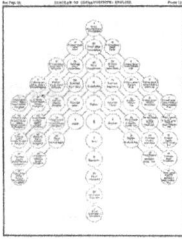

Publication date: 1871.

Author: Lewis Henry Morgan (1818–1881).

Original caption: "Diagram of Consanguinity: English" (Morgan 1871, 604 / Plate III).

This image is discussed in Part III, "Inversions, Continued."

Image in the public domain.

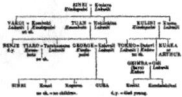

Publication date: 1910.

Author: William Halse Rivers Rivers (1864–1922).

Original caption: "The Genealogical Method of Anthropological Inquiry" (Rivers 1910, 1).

This image is discussed in Part III, "Inversions, Continued."

Image in the public domain.

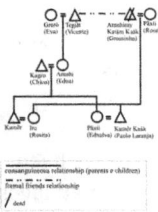

Diagram 7
Formal friends and marriage relations between Tepjêt grandchildren and Amnhimy children

Publication date: 2011.

Author: Odair Giraldin (n.d.).

Original caption: "Formal friends and marriage relations between Tepjêt grandchildren and Amnhimy children" (Giraldin 2011, 421).

In this diagram, Giraldin notes that "we can see that two children of the couple Amnhimy (Grossinho) and Pãxti (Rosa) also married two of Tepjêt (Vicente)'s grandchildren, which demonstrates that the alliance between two people can be extended to a third generation. Amnhimy (Grossinho) and Pãxti (Rosa)'s consanguineous children, Ire (Rosita) and Kamêr Kaàk (Paulo), married children of Kangro (Chico) and Amnhi (Edna) who is Tepjêt and

Grerô's consanguineous daughter. In São Jose, the largest village in Apinaje territory, with an estimated population of 700 (September 1999), I researched one hundred and eight marriages. I verified that in 71 cases there is a relation of formal friendship between one of the spouses and one of the parents-in-law. The result is that 68% of the marriages are or have been in an ideal condition" (Giraldin 2011, 420).

This diagram was published 101 years after Rivers published on the "Genealogical Method" in 1910 (Fig 6.6). Giraldin's diagram differs in appearance — using shapes-as-tropes to denote gender and including dashed lines to denote relationships of "formal friendship" — though in its stated aim to analyze "the link between formal friendship and a matrimonial system among the Apinaje people" (Giraldin 2011, 421), it echoes similar goals to Rivers's earlier work: "[By collecting] a register of the marriages [...] we can see not only what marriages have been allowed or enjoined and what marriages have been prohibited, but we can express statistically the frequency of the different kinds" (Rivers 1910, 6).

Publication date: 1986.
Author: Nancy Munn (1931–2020).
Original caption: "Interhamlet *buwaa* relationships focused in one nodal couple" (Munn 1986, 39).

"Key. ⹀: Neighborhood divisions; ○: Hamlet location; ○ △: Female, male; →: Direction of transaction of female-side gift; 1, 2: Nodal couple; 3, 3a: Foster father and mother of 2; 4, 4a: Foster mother and father of 1; 5, 5a:Dala affiliate brother of 3a (the woman's foster mother) and his wife; 6, 6a: Own mother and father of 1; 7, 7a: Dala brother of 3 (the woman's foster father) and his wife; 8, 8a: Sister of 1 and her husband; 9, 9a: Father and stepmother of 2; 10, 10a: Mother's brother of 1 and the former's wife; 11, 11a: Father's sister's son of 2 and his wife; 12, 12a: Foster father's brother of 1 and the former's wife; 13: Brother ("parallel cousin") of 2; 14, 14a: Sister of 1 and her husband" (Munn 1986, 39).

Munn adapts the established binary tropes of kinship diagrams, wherein each circle or triangle is used to represent a specific woman or man, and modifies the overall layout and format in order to focus analytical attention on specific aspects of social life that exceed the standard genealogical grid of kinship depictions — in this case, interhamlet kinship relations in a Gawan neighborhood.

Used with permission by Cambridge University Press (PLSclear Ref No: 59097).

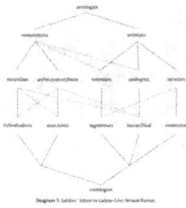

Diagram 3. Sahlins' lattice in Galois–Lévi-Strauss format.

Publication date: 2014.

Author: Mauro William Barbosa de Almeida (n.d.).

Original caption: "Sahlins' lattice in Galois–Lévi-Strauss format" (Almeida 2014, 293).

This diagram "suggests two possible readings [...] one more concerned with 'superstructures,' and the other more along the lines of an 'order of orders' which connects 'superstructures' and 'infrastructures'" (de Almeida 2014, 291). This example echoes a genre of diagrams in anthropology that reflect disciplinary genealogies — variously tracing critical ideas, influential writers, the recognized emergence of concepts or schools of thought, or relationships between any or all of these.

Image used under CC BY-NC-ND.

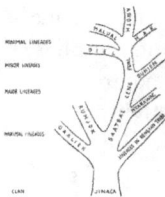

Publication date: 1940.

Author: Edward Evan Evans-Pritchard (1902–1973).

Originally presented without a caption and described in the accompanying text as: "Diagrammatic lineage tree of the Jinaca clan" (Evans-Pritchard 1940, 196).

This image is discussed in Part III, "Inversions, Continued."

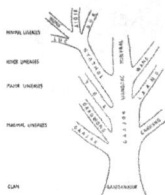

Publication date: 1940.

Author: Edward Evan Evans-Pritchard (1902–1973).

Originally presented without a caption and described in the accompanying text as: "Diagrammatic lineage tree of the

Gaatgankiir clan" (Evans-Pritchard 1940, 197).

This image is discussed in Part III, "Inversions, Continued."

Publication date: 1940.

Author: Edward Evan Evans-Pritchard (1902–1973).

Originally presented without a caption and described in the accompanying text as an illustration of the "The Lineage System" with the following note: "A Nuer clan, therefore, is a system of lineages, the relationship of each lineage to every other lineage being marked in its structure by a point of reference in ascent. The distance to this point is what we call the time depth of a lineage [outline of a Nuer system of lineage]" (Evans-Pritchard 1940, 201).

This image is discussed in Part III, "Inversions, Continued."

Publication date: 1940.

Author: Edward Evan Evans-Pritchard (1902–1973).

Originally presented without a caption and described in the accompanying text as follows: "The relationship between lineage and others of the same clan is not an equal relationship, for lineages are structurally differentiated units which stand to one another at different and exact structural distances [image]. It is interesting to note how the Nuer themselves figure a lineage system. When illustrating on the ground a

number of related lineages they do not present them the way we figure them in this chapter as a series of bifurcations of descent, as a tree of descent, or as a series of triangles of ascent, but as a number of lines running at angles from a common point" (Evans-Pritchard 1940, 202).
This image is discussed in Part III, "Inversions, Continued."

Publication date: 1952.
Author: Melville Jean Herskovits (1895–1963).
Original caption: "Average weekly expenditure per family for various types of food-stuffs and supplies, by Malay of Kalantan (after Rosemary Firth, 181) (Firth 1943)" (Herskovits 1952, 296).
Most diagrams in economic anthropology tend to illustrate modes or relations of trade and transfer — operating at different scales in order to reflect flows of goods, labor, capital, value, commodities, people, or technologies — typically adopting abstractions that remove any human or ecological specificities. This relatively early example anticipates what has since become a more widespread data visualization practice, adding minimal illustration components to straightforward bar graphs or pie charts.
Used with permission by Penguin Random House LLC (Contract #: 52083).

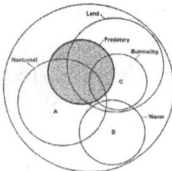

Figure 177 Lele: animals. Characteristics of spirit animals:
A Nocturnal
B Water
C Burrowing

Publication date: 2001 [1975/1999].
Author: Mary Douglas (1921–2007).
Original caption: "Lele: animals.
Characteristics of spirit animals: [A]
Nocturnal; [B] Water; [C] Burrowing"
(Douglas 2001, 271).

Douglas's account of views described by
Lele people living in the Kasai River
region includes the processes by which
human distinction is established through
social rules of shame and avoidance,
in addition to rules signaled by human
spirits, sorcerers, and animal spirits.
There are rules that divide the animal
world into three classes — ordinary
animals, carnivorous animals, and spirit
animals — and different characteristics
of these various animals further
influence the impression, intention,
and enforcement of other social rules.
"The killing and ritual consumption of
specific spirit animals is a central part of
[Lele] prospering rituals. The category
of spirit animals is constituted by two
major criteria, non-predatory and water-
inhabiting (fish and wild pig are prime
examples) and two secondary criteria,
burrowing and nocturnal. These classes
sometimes overlap: nocturnal habits
are a sign of spirit because the spirit
world reverses the order of humans;
burrowing suggests co-habitation with
the dead; water means fertility[. ...]
Whenever a species is allocated by its
observed behaviour to one habitat or
the other, if one of its subspecies by its
behaviour strays into the class of spirit

animals they pay special and favourable attention to the anomalous sub-class. [...] In sum, the Lele are extremely interested in boundary-crossing whenever they observe it" (Douglas 2001, 271–72).
Used with permission by Taylor & Francis Group (Licence PERM3007).

Publication date: 1969
Author: Claude Lévi-Strauss (1908–2009).
Original caption: "Marriage exchanges in Polynesia (after Firth, 1939, 323)" (Lévi-Strauss 1969, 64).
Lévi-Strauss drew on the work of Raymond Firth (1939) to highlight the "astonishing complexity of matrimonial exchanges in Tikopia" (Solomon Islands), which they described as cementing relations between specific groups of "in-laws" and binding each lineage (or kinship group) in "a system of directional exchanges" (Lévi-Strauss 1969, 64).
This image is discussed in Part III, "Inversions, Continued."
"Elementary Structures of Kinship" by Claude Levi-Strauss. Published first in France under the title *Les Structures elementaires de la Parente* in 1949. A revised edition was published under the same title in France in 1967. Translation copyright © 1969 by Beacon Press. Reprinted by permission of Beacon Press, Boston.

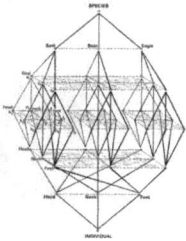

Publication date: 1966.
Author: Claude Lévi-Strauss (1908–2009).
Original caption: "The Totemic Operator"
(Lévi-Strauss 1966, 152).
This notorious image is often, and
understandably, held up as a prime
example of what Alfred Gell (1999)
calls the "excesses" of diagramming
and structuralism, as discussed in
Part III, "Inversions, Continued." The
idea was to imagine a "classification of
classifications" that could account for
the organization of not only different
kinds of classification, such as macro-
and micro-classifications, but also for
the multiple dimensions of binary
classificatory systems themselves,
including animal versus or plant, simple
versus plural, and homogeneous versus
heterogeneous. This is, then, a meta
diagram envisioned as being capable of
expanding without limit and becoming a
"conceptual apparatus" that aids further
classification by filtering "unity through
multiplicity, multiplicity through unity,
diversity through identity, and identity
through diversity" (Lévi-Strauss 1966,
153). Both the utility and the feasibility
of such a project were brought into
question by its author. Lévi-Strauss
concluded that such a classification of
classifications was "perfectly conceivable"
but the sheer number of documents,
dimensions, and data that would have
to be taken into account in order to
manifest it is so vast that such a task was
practically impossible or, at least, "could

not be done without the aid of machines"
(Lévi-Strauss 1966, 151).

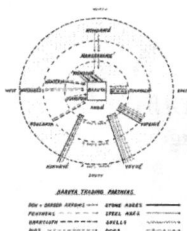

Publication date: 1983.
Author: Allison Jablonko (n.d.) and
Maurice Godelier (b. 1934).
Original caption: "Baruya trading partners"
(Jablonko and Godelier 1983).
This image is discussed in Part III,
"Inversions, Continued."
Used with permission by author Allison
Jablonko.

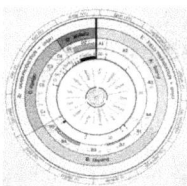

Publication date: 1980.
Author: Harold Colyer Conklin (1926–
2016).
Original caption: "Ifugao calendar year"
(Conklin 1980, 13).
This diagram is just one example of
Conklin's original visual work — a
monumental collection of documentary
and aerial photography, ethnographic
and historic cartography, and analysis
published jointly in 19" x 17" format by
Yale University Press and The American
Geographical Society of New York.
Elaine Gan has more recently revisited
this image and its formal innovations:
"An agricultural year in the Ifugao
mountain provinces of northwestern
Philippines is an interplay of seasonal
activities and synchronized events.
In his *Ethnographic Atlas of Ifugao*,
anthropologist Harold Conklin (1980,
13) diagrams a year as a succession of
events that are intricately coordinated
around the ecology and annual

cultivation of pond-field rice, the most highly valued crop among thousands of plants in Ifugao life. While crop production manuals focus on one end goal, namely harvest for sale, the Ifugao calendar focuses on the coordination and timing of many activities" (Gan 2021, 109–10). Gan adds that the concentric, polyrhythmic calendars that encircle this diagram open up particularly expansive and responsive practices of figuration, inviting further reflection — through diagramming — of multiple "interplays, coordinations, and encounters between rhythms, recursions, and historical trajectories" (ibid.).

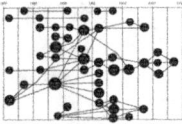

Publication date: 1996.
Author: Roger Neich (1944–2010).
Original caption: "Transmission of selected figurative painting traditions" (Neich 1996, 220).

Gell (1998) discusses both the formal innovation of this diagram and its utility as a contribution to the historical-geographical record: "To what extent can we study the whole gamut of Maori meeting houses, distributed in space and time, as a single, coherent object, distributed in space and time, which, in a certain sense, recapitulates, on the historical and collective scale, the processes of cognition or consciousness? Fortunately, through the very meticulous studies undertaken by Neich, we can indeed make progress in this direction [. ...] The left-to-right axis of the table

corresponds to the axis of historical
time (between 1870 and 1930) while the
top-to-bottom axis, which is unlabelled,
corresponds, implicitly, to geographical
space[. ...] The numbers denote
particular meeting houses in Neich's
comprehensive catalogue of the same,
and the letters correspond to 'traditions'
of Maori figurative painting[. ...] Instead
of arrows, Neich joins the nodal points
in his historico-geographical network
by simple lines; he is not thinking in
terms of protentions and retentions
which, from any given 'now' moment,
or from the temporal standpoint of
any given work of art at the moment of
its completion, always have a definite
directionality, towards the past (memory,
recapitulation) or towards the future
(project, preliminary sketch)[. ...] After
all this, it may seem that Neich has done
well to refrain from using arrows at all"
(Gell 1998, 254–56).
Used with permission by Auckland
University Press.

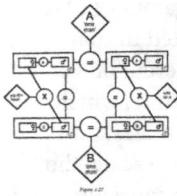

Publication date: 1999.
Author: Alfred A.F. Gell (1945–1997).
Originally presented without a caption
and described in the accompanying text
as an "impossible figure" that reflects
the symbolic practices of marriage
and affinity, particularly the "mutually
irreconcilable appearances of spouse-to-
spouse and affinal-group relations" (Gell
1999, 63–64).

This image is discussed in Part III,
"Inversions, Continued."

Publication date: 1999.
Author: Alfred A.F. Gell (1945–1997).
Originally presented without a caption
and described in the accompanying text
as a "Strathernogram" that details the
specific working and feeding relations
that constitute and support the *dala*
which are "matrilineal sub-clans"
that Gell describes as the "enduring,
self-reproducing, building-blocks of
Trobriand society" (Gell 1999, 70–72).
This image is discussed in Part III,
"Inversions, Continued."

Publication date: 1977.
Author: Pierre Bourdieu (1930–2002).
Original caption: "The abstract 'calendar'"
(Bourdieu 1977, 99).
This image is discussed in Part IV, "Excess
(Possibilities)."
Used with permission by Cambridge
University Press (PLSclear Ref No:
59133).

Publication date: 1977.
Author: Pierre Bourdieu (1930–2002).
Original caption: "The farming year and the
mythical year" (Bourdieu 1977, 134).
This image is discussed in Part IV, "Excess
(Possibilities)."
Used with permission by Cambridge
University Press (PLSclear Ref No:
80779).

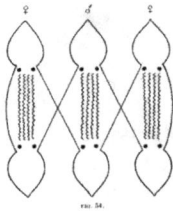

Publication date: 1934.

Author: recreation by Camilla Hildegarde Wedgwood (1901–1955) and Arthur Bernard Deacon (1903–1927).

Original caption: "Three Ghosts" (Deacon and Wedgwood 1934, 163).

As noted in Part IV, "Excess (Possibilities)," some of drawings in this collection compiled by Deacon and Wedgwood were recreated from photographs that Deacon took during fieldwork; others are replications of Deacon's own sketches. However, the original authors and artists responsible for these images are the people whose lives were being documented. Pre-dating 1927, these images remain as century-old examples of using sketching and drawing as praxis within anthropological fieldwork."

Used with permission by Wiley.

Publication date: 1934.

Author: recreation by Camilla Hildegarde Wedgwood (1901–1955) and Arthur Bernard Deacon (1903–1927).

Original caption: "Adultery" (Deacon and Wedgwood 1934, 161).

This image is discussed in Part IV, "Excess (Possibilities)."

Used with permission by Wiley.

Publication date: undated.

Author: Mitch Miller (n.d.).

Original caption: "Drawing of the Niven's Flat: The Nivens from S(i)even was put together with the kind help and assistance of the Niven family, residents of the [Red Road Flats] scheme for 40 years. The Nivens moved out in 2008, and their flat is long gone but, with the aid of Bob Niven, whose memory is somewhat encyclopaedic, I was able to reconstruct his family home as best I could" (Miller n.d., n.p.).

Miller's ongoing experiments with visual forms even more explicitly incorporated research processes into the presented images. "Glasgow Dialectograms explore the use of illustration as record, information as art. Superficially a pastiche of scientific, anthropological and architectural illustrations, Dialectograms comment upon contemporary city spaces, public, private and personal, through creating an extremely detailed schematic of a place that condenses and includes both subjective and objective information into a single piece. They show facts, thoughts and feelings. They use a deliberately loose and organic 'anti-architectural' drawing style to describe not just what it is there, but who uses it, what a particular space means to someone, and how relationships between people shape their environment. The term 'Psycho-Geography' applies, but put simply, they are made by talking to people, sharing ideas and processing them into visual forms — a diagram, a dialogue, a dialectic, but also a dialect of technical drawing — hence, Dialectogram" (Miller n.d., n.p.).

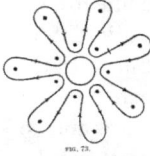

Publication date: 1934.
Author: recreation by Camilla Hildegarde Wedgwood (1901–1955) and Arthur Bernard Deacon (1903–1927).
Original caption: "Drop of Water" (Deacon and Wedgwood 1934, 170).
This image is discussed in Part IV, "Excess (Possibilities)."
Used with permission by Wiley.

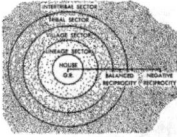

Publication date: 1972.
Author: Marshall Sahlins (1930–2021).
Original caption: "Reciprocity and Kinship Residential Sectors" (Sahlins 1972, 199).
This image is discussed in Part IV, "Excess (Possibilities)."

Publication date: 2000 [1992].
Author: Deborah Bird Rose (1946–2018).
Original caption: "Sixteen subsection categories showing circles of women, brothers and marriage partners [Yarralin marriage practices and identities cross-cutting moieties and social categories]" (Rose 2000, 77).
This image is discussed in Part IV, "Excess (Possibilities)."
Used with permission by Cambridge University Press (PLSclear Ref No: 59062).

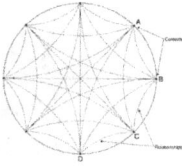

Publication date: 2000 [1992].
Author: Deborah Bird Rose (1946–2018).
Original caption: "Relationships and
Contexts" (Rose 2000, 222).
This image is discussed in Part IV, "Excess
(Possibilities)."
Used with permission by Cambridge
University Press (PLSclear Ref No:
59073).

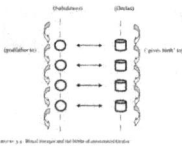

Publication date: 2012.
Author: Martin Holbraad (n.d.).
Original caption: "Ritual lineages and the
births of consecrated Orulas" (Holbraad
2012, 95).
This image is discussed below.
Used with permission by University of
Chicago Press, all rights reserved (ref.
00495312127). Holbraad, M., 2012. *Truth
in Motion: The Recursive Anthropology of
Cuban Divination.* Chicago: University
of Chicago Press.

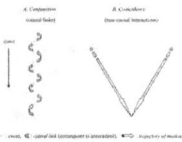

Publication date: 2012.
Author: Martin Holbraad (n.d.).
Original caption: "Conjunction ('how') as
causation and coincidence ('why') as
non-causal motility" (Holbraad 2012,
199).
Holbraad further emphasizes: "A key point
to note, somewhat abstractly for now,
is that coincidences involve interaction.
Coincidental relations do not pan out as
ordered series like causal ones do, but
are rather constituted at the *intersections*
of causal series, as illustrated in [this
figure]. From this it follows that the

points of intersection that constitute coincidental relations correspond to events, since they represent meeting-points of series that are in motion. Since causal chains themselves comprise events — that is, alterations over time — their meetings properly constitute temporary collisions of trajectories. One may say, then, that coincidences are best glossed oxymoronically as non-causal interactions, or, more poetically, as *pure effects*" (Holbraad 2012, 199).

Explored through his book on Cuban practices of divination, Holbraad's broader project concerns anthropology as a question of "how to make sense of others" — but mobilized specifically by questions of the impossibility of representation, where alterity itself is understood as that which cannot be represented and the goal is an "anthropology beyond representation" (Holbraad 2012, xvi). These original approaches to figuration — of both genealogical, philosophical, or causal information — are striking in part for their simultaneous augmentation of and adherence to linear, diagrammatic logics established much earlier in anthropology (for example in the work of Evans-Pritchard).

Used with permission by University of Chicago Press, all rights reserved (ref. 00495312127).

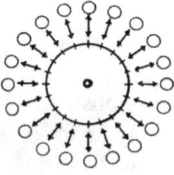

Publication date: 1988.

Author: Jadran Mimica (n.d.).

Original caption: "Mapping the wholes onto the base of 20 parts" (Mimica 1988, 71).

This image is discussed below under the next figure.

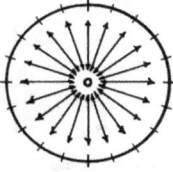

Publication date: 1988.

Author: Jadran Mimica (n.d.).

Original caption: "Self-referential mapping" (Mimica 1988, 71).

Mimica offers the complex interpretation of ideas described by Iqwaye people concerning relationships between personhood (persons partially correlating with the significance of each base set of twenty digits); counting and enumeration (where addition also means transference into a new sets of relations); infinity; and the mythopoeic meanings of procreation which also relates to bases sets of twenty digits, where "each hand is a bisexual male procreative whole, in relation to which fingers are its male and female children" (Mimica 1988, 70–71). Within these systems, figure 6.34 represents the notion of genitor in relation to their children, each of which are sets of twenties, and figure 6.35 represents the notion of an individual in which base parts maps onto a single self, through "complete identification" and thereby "effecting their totalisation" (Mimica 1988, 70).

Publication date: 1936.

Author: John Willoughby Layard (1891–1974).

Original caption: "(Layard, unpublished, from Atchin [island]): Two flying foxes [i.e. ghosts] eating bread fruit. Note the division of the figure and the substitution of spirals for dots or circles" (Layard 1936, 150).

This image is one of more than a hundred that Layard compiled and recreated, showing a style of continuous-line sand drawings established in Malekula Island, Vanuatu.

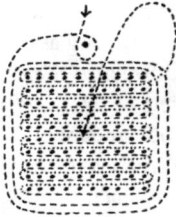

Publication date: 1936.

Author: John Willoughby Layard (1891–1974).

Original caption: "The Hawk pouncing on its prey" (Layard 1936, 158).

This image is another of the "continuous-line designs" that Layard reproduces, but this time specifically the style of work that documents Malekulan dances, images that themselves fulfill both documentary and aesthetic ends. Gell (1998, 94) cites this image (figure 6.37) — in which dots represent dancers, arrows indicate the direction in which they are facing, and the broken lines represent the paths they trace in dancing — as evidence of Layard's interest in and insights into something that would have been "utterly foreign to the mind-set of his anthropological contemporaries," namely the "affinity between the choreography of Malakulan dance and the style of their graphic art." This idea Gell then traces through broader processes of evaluation of plastic (i.e., sculptural) arts in other cultural contexts, reflecting on what we might learn or notice anew when we consider acts of drawing as "akin" to dancing (Gell 1998, 94).

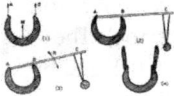

Publication date: 1922.
Author: Bronisław Malinowski (1884–1942).
Original caption: "Diagram showing in transversal section some principles of canoe stability and construction" (Malinowski 1922, 83).
This image is discussed below under the next figure.
Image in the public domain.

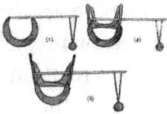

Publication date: 1922.
Author: Bronisław Malinowski (1884–1942).
Original caption: "Diagrammatic sections of the three types of Trobriand Canoe: (1) Kewo'u [upper left]; (2) Kalipoulo [upper right]; (3) Masawa" (Malinowski 1922, 85).

Malinowski used diagrams with cartographic purposes and also within his work on linguistics, but these cross-sectional drawings of canoes fulfill more documentary purposes — illustrating different types of vessels. Given Malinowski's long shadow over anthropology, it is interesting to note how he frames such documentary work — as of minimal impact, use, or accuracy when presented without accompanying, and extensive, ethnographic details: "A canoe is an item of material culture, and as such it can be described, photographed and even bodily transported into a museum. But — and this is a truth too often overlooked — the ethnographic reality of the canoe would not be brought much nearer to a student at home, even by placing a perfect specimen right before [them]" (Malinowski 1922, 105). The object, by itself, is merely fetishized by any outside observer. Malinowski adds that even "further sociological data" concerning ownership of, purposes for, planned routes for, and techniques of using canoes, or even information "regarding the ceremonies and customs of its construction" (Malinowski 1922, 105) are all insufficient for helping any reader to grasp the depth of resonance of canoes for those living in direct relation with them. In Malinowski's work, then, diagrams, and the visual and material that they stand in for, are but one contributing element to ethnographic work that seeks to meaningfully engage in understanding the emotional relationships that connect particular people with certain resonant objects. Image in the public domain.

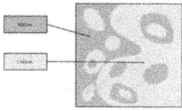

Publication date: 2018.

Author: John Law (n.d.) and Marianne Lien (n.d.).

Original caption: "The mutual inclusion of nature and culture" (Law and Lien 2018, 148).

As indicated by this figure, "overlaps, tensions, and paradoxes all suggest that the picture we need to draw if we want to visualize the boundaries between nature and culture will often take [this] form of mutual inclusion" (Law and Lien 2018, 148). This image is one of a series of ten different ways of visualizing relationships between nature and culture presented by Law and Lien in their chapter on "denaturalizing nature" for the volume *A World of Many Worlds*. In this chapter they build out from a Latourian basis that modernity is "both coherent and not coherent at all" in order to scrutinize how the "science of a singular world" (Law and Lien 2018, 149) is persistently and powerfully reproduced, taking as their case the farming of salmon in Norway. This figure is deceptively simple. The series of which it forms a part summarizes a range of ways of understanding human/nonhuman mutuality, critiques of conceptual modernity, and ontological politics.

Republished with permission by Duke University Press (ref. DUP-RP-5262).

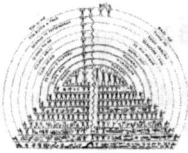

Publication date: 1919.

Author: Paiore, in a publication by J. L. Young (n.d.).

Original caption: "The Paumotu Conception of the Heavens" (Young 1919, 210b).

The editors of the *Journal of Polynesian Society* that originally published this image added the following note: "Through the courtesy of Mr. Young we are enabled to reproduce a quite unique drawing made by Paiore, a man from the Paumotu Group, in 1869, representing the world, and the heavens above as conceived of by the branch of the Polynesians to which Paiore belonged" (Young 1919, 209). That text includes a translation of a statement made by the original artist, dating the work to fifty years before its institutional publication: "The likeness (or description) of things made known to the people of ancient times. The form of this our World and the account of our ancestors, and of the beginning of the movement of animal life. This is the true and succinct description [literally a bundle tied up with a knotted string] of mankind which was confined in narrow spaces, and of the origin of things and of the various trees [or vegetation] and of the bringing forth of animals which suckle their young, such as four-footed animals. These are to be seen in this sheet of paper as understood by the writer, I, Paiore, 1869" (Young 1919, 210a).

As a reproduction of someone else's
work — the publication of a research
participant's drawing — this piece is a
precursor to the images, above, compiled
by Deacon and Wedgwood, and a further
example of diagrams as documentary
work and of visual mediations playing
critical roles within fieldwork processes.
Image in the public domain.

Publication date: 2021.
Author: Max Liboiron (n.d.), after Mary
Douglas (1921–2007).
Original caption: "The four myths of
Nature: (A) Nature is capricious: the
ball can roll anywhere, anytime; (B)
Nature is fragile: the ball can roll off at
any moment!; (C) Nature is robust: that
ball is not going anywhere; (D) Nature is
robust within limits: the ball will roll out
if we push too hard. Illustration by Max
Liboiron. CC-BY 3.0" (Liboiron 2021, 61).
These four myth-schematics are slightly
modified versions of the same diagrams
that first appeared in Mary Douglas's
1992 book *Risk and Blame: Essays
in Cultural Theory* (they appear as
figure 14.1 in the republished edition,
Douglas 2003, 263). The four images
depict four different cultural views of
nature. Douglas links each of the four
to cultural patterns in social relations
among different types or groups: (A) is
linked to what she terms Fatalists; (B)
to Communards; (C) to Entrepreneurial
Expansionists; and (D) to Hierarchists.
Building out from these points in

new directions, Liboiron outlines the consequences of when dominant societal views embrace model (D) — nature as robust within limits — along with attendant threshold theories of harm. Liboiron notes that "land relations become managerial rather than reciprocal. In colonial understandings of Nature, (certain) humans can protect, extend, augment, better, use, preserve, destroy, interrupt, and/or capitalize on robust-within-limits Nature [D]. That is, Land becomes a Resource. Resources refer to unidirectional relations where aspects of land are useful to particular (here, settler and colonial) ends. In this unidirectional relation, value flows in one direction, from the Resource to the user, rather than being reciprocal" (Liboiron 2021, 62).

Image used under CC BY 3.0.

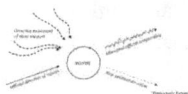

Publication date: 2016.
Author: Eli Thorkelson (n.d.).
Original caption: "[still from] Video 2: A schematic diagram of disruption in official temporality" (Thorkelson 2016, 507).

The creativity of this piece cannot be fully captured in a single image. This is a still image from an animated diagram that depicts political disruption over time and according to institutional notions of temporality. The original article contains a link to the animated work.

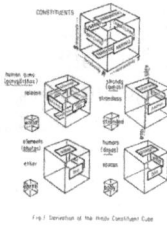

Fig / Derivation of the Hindu Constituent Cube

Publication date: 1989.

Author: McKim Marriott (1924–2024).

Original caption: "Derivation of the Hindu Constituent Cube" (Marriott 1989, 10). This complex diagram was accompanied by specific notes on both its formal and figurative contents: "Since the cubes are not intended to imply static substance or impenetrability, they are drawn as transparent[. ...] All cubes are more or less open to movements between their internal and external spaces, and none is intended to provide an exhaustive accounting of the sphere that it depicts. Three-dimensional graphing opens the possibility that differing points of view may explain the differing conventional orders for listing the faces of what may still be a single underlying shape" (Marriott 1989, 9–11).

Marriott referenced his audience in presenting these images, recognizing that certain mathematical conventions of graphing — and the familiarity of the cube — might be more suited to "scholars used to living in and with such structures" (Marriott 1989, 9). Marriott also acknowledged the tensions surrounding such choices, particularly when he cited an underlying motivation as an attempt to denounce the "imperial style of Western ethnosocial science" and the imposition of its own ontological and epistemological concepts onto others. The cube shape is adopted as a means for moving beyond the "insistent

dualizing" of "Western topologies"
and for exploring graphic forms that
might reflect more closely the multi-
dimensionality of multiple qualities or
guna (strands), *dosas* (humors), *bhutas*
(elements) and other aspects at play
within Hindu cosmologies: "[C]ubes are
therefore offered here provisionally as
geometric metaphors and mnemonics
for Indian spaces within which
everything must be rated along at least
three different dimensions" (Marriott
1989, 9).

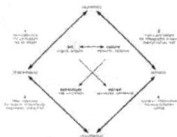

Publication date: 1988.
Author: James Clifford (b. 1945).
Original caption: "The Art-Culture System:
A Machine for Making Authenticity"
(Clifford 1988, 224).
"The Pure Products Go Crazy[. ... There's]
no one to drive the car." Clifford opens
his 1988 book with these words, quoting
at length a poem by William Carlos
Williams as a pretext for the essays that
follow and as a way of "starting in with
a predicament" — the predicament of
"ethnographic modernity" (Clifford 1988,
3). Contested meanings and contested
values are the recurrent themes that
then re-appear in the form of this
diagram — or "map" as he describes
it: "[T]he following map [... is] of a
historically specific, contestible field of
meanings and institutions. Beginning
with an initial opposition, by a process of
negation four terms are generated. This
establishes horizontal and vertical axes

and between them four semantic zones:
(1) the zone of authentic masterpieces,
(2) the zone of authentic artifacts, (3)
the zone of inauthentic masterpieces,
(4) the zone of inauthentic artifacts.
Most objects — old and new, rare and
common, familiar and exotic — can
be located in one of these zones or
ambiguously, in traffic, between two
zones. The system classifies objects and
assigns them relative value" (Clifford
1988, 223). While its contents and
implications are clearly contestable,
arguably it is everything that the map or
diagram fails to incorporate that makes it
useful, as Clifford himself suggests.
Beyond its apparent initial utility as a
way to dissect notions of the "exotic"
and the "artistic," and their relative
markers — beauty, originality,
value — there are also multiple ways
of applying and interpreting the
routes that these arrows imply. The
text emphasizes how these differently
mapped "contexts" allow for different
negotiations, exchanges, and circulations
of objects. And it is here that the author's
disclaimers invite further exploration:
of how the "art-culture system" he has
diagrammed "excludes and marginalizes
various residual and emergent contexts"
such as religious objects; of how this
same system cannot escape its own
"historicity," that positions and values
assigned to artifacts will continue
to change over time; and of what is
occluded by "a synchronic diagram"

which "cannot represent zones of contest and transgression except as movements or ambiguities among fixed poles" (Clifford 1988, 226).

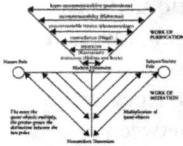

Publication date: 1993.

Author: Bruno Latour (1947–2022).

Original caption: "The modern paradox" (Latour 1993, 58).

With this image, Latour references both the visualized and the implied, the explicitly stated and the implicitly placed: "Once again the modern paradox is taken further. The notion of intentionality transforms a distinction, a separation, a contradiction, into an insurmountable tension between object and subject. The hopes of dialectics are abandoned, since this tension offers no resolution. The phenomenologists have the impression that they have gone further than Kant and Hegel and Marx, since they no longer attribute any essence either to pure subjects or to pure objects. They really have the impression that they are speaking only of a mediation that does not require any pole to hold fast. Yet like so many anxious modernizers, they no longer trace anything but a line between poles that are thus given the greatest importance. Pure objectivity and pure consciousness are missing, but they are nevertheless — indeed, all the more — in place." (Latour 1993, 58).

Though the insight did not deter him from creating this particular image, Latour was well aware of the potential

for diagrams to become complex to
a point of inscrutability: "Diagrams,
lists, formulae, archives, engineering
drawings, files, equations, dictionaries,
collections and so on, depending on
the way they are put into focus, may
explain almost everything or almost
nothing" (Latour 1986, 4). The point of
focus here may remain indistinct, but
it is not limited to the preoccupations
of phenomenologists. Rather, it is a
perhaps still impenetrable attempt to
identify grades of comparison among
the "major modern philosophies" which
share three strategies for absorbing both
the modern nature and society divide
and an acknowledgment of social,
nonhuman "quasi-objects" that exist
"between and below" the two poles. "The
first [strategy] consists in establishing a
great gap between objects and subjects
and continually increasing the distance
between them; the second, known as the
'semiotic turn', focuses on the middle and
abandons the extremes; the third isolates
the idea of Being, thus rejecting the
whole divide between objects, discourse
and subjects" (Latour 1993, 55–56).

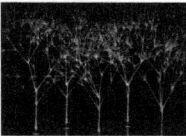

Publication date: 2012.
Author: Agnes Chavez (n.d.).
Original caption: "(x)trees data
    visualization screenshot of an algorithm"
    (Chavez 2012, n.p.).
This image provides a glimpse of data-
    driven, computer-assisted diagram

design. "(x)trees is a dynamically generating forest of trees created from SMS and Tweets from the audience in real time. It is projected in real time on to buildings and large spaces, exploring our relationship to nature and technology. (x)trees tours around the world creating a participatory experience to raise awareness to ecological topics such as deforestation and climate change. By integrating data mining from SMS and social networks, people participate in the creation of the branches to form a virtual interactive forest of dynamically generating trees. The audience sends a tweet or text message and sees their message appear on the wall with a branch. Archived messages include articles from the Universal Declaration of Rights for Mother Earth and the Outer Space Treaty of 1967" (Chavez 2012, n.p.).

Image: (x)trees data visualization screenshot of algorithm (Chavez 2012), as published in Ruppert (2016), CC BY-NC-SA 4.0.

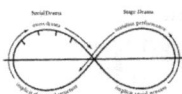

Publication date: 1985.

Author: Victor Turner (1920–1983).

Original caption: "The interrelationship of social drama and stage drama" (Turner 1985, 300).

This diagram was accompanied by specific notes on its formal structure: "The two semicircles above the horizontal dividing line represent the manifest, visible public realm. The left loop or circlet represents social drama, which could be divided into its four main phases: breach, crisis, redress, positive or negative denouement. The right loop represents a genre of cultural performance — in this case, a stage of 'aesthetic' drama (though it would be better to say the total repertoire of types of cultural performance possessed by a society)" (Turner 1985, 300).

Turner's account of social and stage drama interrelationships is referenced in now countless re-assessments of how we understand a range of social phenomena: from directly related realms of ritual, religion, theater, play, games, competition, and performance, through theoretical questions concerning liminality, efficacy, the spectacular, selfhood, and individuality, and on to the application of these reimaginings within diverse social processes such as healthcare provision or the consumption of food. The fact that this diagram is so well traveled partly reflects the illustrative utility of the infinite loop: everything is interrelated, change is movement, movement is endless, and all processes connect.

Publication date: 2015 [1982].
Author: Christopher A. Gregory (n.d.).
Original caption: "The minor 1964–1974 *moka* chains: initiatory sequence" (Gregory 2015, 58). Gregory's work details what he calls "roads of gift-debt": the circulation of gifts of different "rank" and "velocity" which has the

effect of bind binding people together in "complicated webs of gift-debt" (Gregory 2015, 57). The figure depicts "the minor roads that fed into the initiatory sequence of the main road, and [the next figure] shows the minor roads that fed into (and led off) the return sequence along the main road" (Gregory 2015, 58). These two diagrams show the "minor roads" of exchange that formed the outward (fig. 6.49) and return (fig. 6.50) sequences of exchange and emphasize the importance of timing: in both sequences C was a major junction, whose gifts depended on the prior receipt of goods and gifts from others, which in turn were dependent on the prior return of offerings from still other parties (Gregory 2015, 59).
Used with permission by image author.

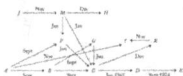

Publication date: 2015 [1982].
Author: Christopher A. Gregory (n.d.).
Original caption: "The minor 1964–1974 moka chains: return sequence" (Gregory 2015, 59).
Together, figures 6.49 and 6.50 stem from Gregory's work seeking to intervene in debates of the era on some of the discipline's persistent concerns: exchange, reciprocity, reproduction, and theories of the gift and of the commodity. Their design reflects a preoccupation with socioeconomics, a focus that, both regionally and conceptually, would be changed with the publication of Marilyn Strathern's

The Gender of the Gift (1988): "Whereas my book addresses 1970s debates in political economy and economic anthropology, her book addresses 1980s cross-disciplinary debates about gender" (Gregory 2015, xxvi). These were thematic shifts that invited more critical work on gender and, from there, on the body, selfhood, personhood, subjectivity, and autonomy (Strathern 2015) — work which itself became the focus of more visual anthropological thinking, such as the "Strathernograms" by Gell (1999), discussed in Part III, "Inversions, Continued."

Used with permission by image author.

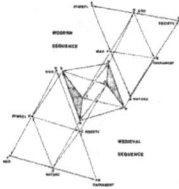

Publication date: 1986.

Author: Roy Wagner (1938–2018).

Original caption: "The medieval-modern reversal"(Wagner 1986, 123).

This complex image (which is also today somewhat infamous as an example of diagrammatic excess) combines theoretical approaches that connect anthropological and psychological concerns: "The medieval trope was an expression of continual and cumulative reform and refinement of received scriptural revelation, against the resistance of an internally generated collectivism. [...] The modem trope, by contrast, had put its reform, in the Reformation, behind it; it was motivated by a compulsion of forward-directed implication (like the compulsion of the *habu*) rather than a resistance[. ...]

The best analytic example is Weber's account of the Protestant ethic and its transformation into the spirit of capitalism. The Calvinists' notion of predestination was not medieval, but part of the internal, dialectically produced hierarchicism of the modem sequence. [...] The medieval and modem tropes each replicated the other as an internal, motivating factor because, basically, each trope is formed against the other. This is the significance of the figure-ground reversal. Taken as a whole, the meaning of this double trope is involute: it generates its own referential space, stands for itself, and is about itself" (Wagner 1986, 122–23). Expanding his discussion of the figure-ground reversal, adopted from gestalt psychology and applied to explore the construction and operation of meaning — specifically as a matter of perception — Wagner deploys a series of diagrams that are often maligned for their impenetrability, but which arguably align with his explorations of the "elicitative nature of trope" and a commitment to the "elicitory" in addition to the more readily recognizable "theoretical" (Wagner 1986, x).

Used with permission by University of Chicago Press, all rights reserved (ref. 00495312127).

Map Drawn by Kazoola. (1) Tarkar Village. (2) Dahomey's Land. (3) Wavering line showing stealthy march of Dahomeyans through forest. (4) Route by which captive Tarkars were taken to the sea. (5), (6), (7), (8), Eko, Budigree, Adaché, Whydah, towns through which Tarkars passed. (9) River. (10) Beach and sea.

Publication date: 1914.

Author: Cudjoe Lewis (c.1841–1935), in a publication by Emma Langdon Roche (1878–1945).

Original caption: "Map Drawn by Kazoola: (1) Tarkar Village. (2) Dahomey's Land. (3) Wavering line showing stealthy march of Dahomeyans through forest. (4) Route by which captive Tarkars were taken to the sea. (5), (6), (7), (8), Eko, Budigree, Adaché, Whydah, towns through which Tarkars passed. (9) River. (10) Beach and sea" (Langdon Roche 1914, 88).

Cudjoe/Cudjo Lewis (born Oluale Kossola, also known as Kazoola) was, at the time, one of the last living survivors of those who had been forced into slavery and trafficked across the Atlantic from Ouidah, on the west coast of Africa, to Alabama via forty-five days on the Clotilda ship; he became a long-time participant in the work of Zora Neale Hurston (Cep 2018, n.p.).

As editor for the 2018 edition of Hurston's *Barracoon: The Story of the Last "Black Cargo,"* Deborah Plant cites how Hurston addressed naming and attribution for this drawing: "[I] went to talk to Cudjo Lewis. That is the American version of his name. His African name was Kossola-O-Lo-Loo-Ay" (Hurston 1942, 198). Plant also notes that elsewhere Hurston transcribed this name as "Kossula" and "Kazoola," while in the more recent research of Sylviane Diouf the preferred spelling is "Kossola,"

191

since this is a name "immediately
decipherable" to the Isha Yoruba people
of West Africa who "have a town named
Kossola" (Diouf 2007, 40; cited in
Hurston 2018, 156).
Tracing the life of Cudjoe Lewis in detail,
Diouf describes this map drawn by him
as "highly problematic and unreliable"
due to research practice at the time,
yet also still of use in establishing
his biography and connecting his
experiences with those of his peers
and community members (Diouf 2007,
40). While raising critical questions
around research methods and ethics,
the map remains an important example
of drawing-as-testimony and of
diagrammatic work as documentary
work.
Image in the public domain.

References

Adams, Tim. 1996. "Diagrams of Interface, or, Deleuze and
    Guattari's Legacy to Architects." Conference presentation,
    A Deleuzian Century (symposium), University of Western
    Australia, Sydney, Australia. December 5–7.

Adorno, Theodor W. 1973. *Negative Dialectics.* Translated by
    E.B. Ashton. New York: Continuum.

Alexander, Christopher. 1979. *Notes on the Synthesis of Form.*
    Cambridge: Harvard University Press.

Almeida, Mauro William Barbosa de. 2014. "Diagrams."
    HAU: Journal of Ethnographic Theory 4, no. 1: 291–94. DOI:
    10.14318/hau4.1.014.

Augé, Marc. 1995. *Non-Places: An Introduction to an
    Anthropology of Supermodernity.* Translated by John Howe.
    London: Verso.

Azoulay, Ariella. 2019. *Potential History: Unlearning
    Imperialism.* London: Verso.

Banks, Marcus. 2001. *Visual Methods in Social Research.*
    London: Sage.

Barnard, Alan, and Anthony Good. 1984. *Research Practices in
    the Study of Kinship.* London: Academic Press.

Barnes, John A. 1967. "Genealogies." In *The Craft of Social
    Anthropology,* edited by Arnold Epstein, 101–28. London:
    Tavistock.

Bender, John B., and Michael Marrinan. 2010. *The Culture of Diagram*. Stanford: Stanford University Press.

Benjamin, Andrew. 1998. "Lines of Work: Notes on Diagrams." *ANY: Architecture New York* 23: 36–39. https://www.jstor.org/stable/41856100.

Berkel, Ben van, and Caroline Bos. 1998. "Diagrams: Interactive Instruments in Operation." *ANY: Architecture New York* 23: 19–23. https://www.jstor.org/stable/41856095.

Bertin, Jacques. 2010. *Semiology of Graphics: Diagrams, Networks, Maps*. Translated by William J. Berg. Redlands: ESRI Press.

Bialecki, Jon. 2016. "Diagramming the Will: Ethics and Prayer, Text, and Politics." *Ethnos* 81, no. 4: 712–34. DOI: 10.1080/00141844.2014.986151.

———. 2017. *A Diagram for Fire: Miracles and Variation in an American Charismatic Movement*. Berkeley: University of California Press.

Bird-David, Nurit. 2019. "Dis/Working with Diagrams: How Genealogies and Maps Obscure Nanoscale Worlds (a Hunter-Gatherer Case)." *Social Analysis* 63, no. 4: 43–62. DOI: 10.3167/sa.2019.630403.

Bonilla, Yarimar. 2015. *Non-Sovereign Futures: French Caribbean Politics in the Wake of Disenchantment*. Chicago: University of Chicago Press. DOI: 10.7208/chicago/9780226283951.001.0001.

Bosteels, Bruno. 1998. "From Text to Territory: Félix Guattari's Cartographies of the Unconscious." In *Deleuze and Guatarri: New Mappings in Politics, Philosophy, and Culture*, edited by Eleanor Kaufman and Kevin Jon Heller, 145–74. Minneapolis: University of Minnesota Press.

Bouquet, Mary. 1995. "Exhibiting Knowledge: The Trees of Dubois, Haeckel, Jesse and Rivers at the *Pithecanthropus* Centennial Exhibition." In *Shifting Contexts: Transformations in Anthropological Knowledge*, edited by Marilyn Strathern, 31–55. London: Routledge.

———. 1996. "Family Trees and Their Affinities: The Visual Imperative of the Genealogical Diagram." *The Journal of the Royal Anthropological Institute* 2, no. 1: 43–66. DOI: 10.2307/3034632.

Bourdieu, Pierre. 1977. *Outline of a Theory of Practice.* Translated by Richard Nice. Cambridge: Cambridge University Press.

———. 1990. *The Logic of Practice.* Translated by Richard Nice. Cambridge: Polity Press.

Brinkema, Eugenie. 2022. *Life-Destroying Diagrams.* Durham: Duke University Press.

Candea, Matei. 2019. "On Visual Coherence and Visual Excess: Writing, Diagrams, and Anthropological Form." *Social Analysis* 63, no. 4: 63–88. DOI: 10.3167/sa.2019.630404.

Carsten, Janet. 2004. *After Kinship.* Cambridge: Cambridge University Press.

Carver, Louise. 2023. "Seeing No Net Loss: Making Nature Offset-able." *Environment and Planning E: Nature and Space* 6, no. 4: 2182–202. DOI: 10.1177/25148486211063732.

Cep, Casey. 2018. "Zora Neale Hurston's Story of a Former Slave Finally Comes to Print." *The New Yorker,* May 7. https://www.newyorker.com/magazine/2018/05/14/zora-neale-hurstons-story-of-a-former-slave-finally-comes-to-print.

Certeau, Michel de. 1984. *The Practice of Everyday Life.* Translated by Steven Rendall. Berkeley: University of California Press.

Chavez, Agnes. 2012. "(X)trees: A Dynamically Generating Forest of Trees from SMS and Tweets." *Agnes.Chavez.* https://agneschavez.com/portfolio/xtrees/.

Clifford, James. 1988. *The Predicament of Culture: Twentieth Century Ethnography, Literature, and Art.* Cambridge: Harvard University Press.

———. 2005. "Rearticulating Anthropology." In *Unwrapping the Sacred Bundle: Reflections on the Disciplining of Anthropology,* edited by Daniel A. Segal and Sylvia J. Yanagisako, 24–48. Durham: Duke University Press. DOI: 10.2307/j.ctv125jm8d.4.

Colloredo-Mansfeld, Rudi. 2011. "Space, Line and Story in the Invention of an Andean Aesthetic." *Journal of Material Culture* 16, no. 1: 3–23. DOI: 10.1177/1359183510394945.

Conklin, Harold, Puggūwon Lupāih, and Miklos Pinther. 1980. *Ethnographic Atlas of Ifugao: A Study of Environment, Culture, and Society in Northern Luzon.* New Haven: Yale University Press.

Conley, Tom. 2011. "Deleuze and the Filmic Diagram." *Deleuze Studies* 5, no. 2: 163–76. https://www.jstor.org/stable/45331457.

Cournot, Antoine Augustin. 1922. *Essai sur les fondements de nos connaissances et sur les caractères de la critique philosophique.* Paris: Hachette.

Crick, Malcolm. 1982. "Anthropological Field Research, Meaning Creation and Knowledge Construction." In *Semantic Anthropology,* edited by David Parkin, 15–37. London: Academic Press.

Das, Veena. 2012. "Intersection: Economies of Knowledge." In *Differentiating Development: Beyond an Anthropology of Critique,* edited by Soumhya Venkatesan and Thomas Yarrow, 58–62. New York: Berghahn Books. DOI: 10.1515/9780857453044-005.

Daston, Lorraine, and Peter Galison. 1992. "The Image of Objectivity." *Representations* 40: 81–128. DOI: 10.2307/2928741.

Davies, Colin, and Monika Parrinder. 2004. "Shooting Images: Photographs from the War in Iraq." *Things Magazine* 17–18 (Spring). https://thingsmagazine.net/text/t17/sontagA.htm.

Davis, Mike. 1999. *Ecology of Fear: Los Angeles and the Imagination of Disaster.* New York: Vintage.

De Landa, Manuel. 1998. "Deleuze, Diagrams, and the Genesis of Form." *ANY: Architecture New York* 23: 30–34. https://www.jstor.org/stable/41856098.

Deacon, A. Bernard, and Camilla H. Wedgwood. 1934. "Geometrical Drawings from Malekula and Other Islands of the New Hebrides." *The Journal of the Royal Anthropological*

Institute of Great Britain and Ireland 64: 129–75. DOI: 10.2307/2843952.

Deleuze, Gilles. 1988. *Foucault.* Translated by Seán Hand. Minneapolis: University of Minnesota Press.

———. 2003. *Francis Bacon: The Logic of Sensation.* London: Continuum.

Deleuze, Gilles, and Félix Guattari. 1987. *A Thousand Plateaus: Capitalism and Schizophrenia.* Translated by Brian Massumi. Minneapolis: University of Minnesota Press.

Derrida, Jacques. 1995. "Archive Fever: A Freudian Impression." Translated by Eric Prenowitz. *Diacritics* 25, no. 2: 9–63. DOI: 10.2307/465144.

Dewey, John. 1934. *Art As Experience.* New York: Minton, Balch & Co.

Diouf, Sylviane A. 2007. *Dreams of Africa in Alabama: The Slave Ship Clotilda and the Story of the Last Africans Brought to America.* Oxford: Oxford University Press.

Doruff, Sher. 2009. "The Tendency to 'Trans-': The Political Aesthetics of the Biogrammatic Zone." In *Interfaces of Performance,* edited by Maria Chatzichristodoulou, Janis Jefferies, and Rachel Zerihan, 121–40. Farnham: Ashgate.

Douglas, Mary. 2002. *Implicit Meanings: Selected Essays in Anthropology.* London: Routledge. DOI: 10.4324/9780203029909.

———. 2003. *Risk and Blame: Essays in Cultural Theory.* London: Routledge.

Douglas-Jones, Rachel. 2021. "Drawing as Analysis: Thinking in Images, Writing in Words." In *Experimenting with Ethnography: A Companion to Analysis,* edited by Andrea Ballestero and Brit Ross Winthereik, 94–105. Durham: Duke University Press. DOI: 10.1215/9781478013211-010.

Du Bois, William Edward Burghardt. 1900a. *[The Georgia Negro] Assessed value of household and kitchen furniture owned by Georgia Negroes.* Drawing, ink and wash, 710 × 560 mm (board). Washington: US Library of Congress. https://www.loc.gov/pictures/item/2013650445/.

————. 1900b. *[The Georgia Negro] Assessed valuation of of all taxable property owned by Georgia Negroes.* Drawing, ink and watercolor, 710 × 560 mm (board). Washington: US Library of Congress. https://www.loc.gov/pictures/item/2013650442/.

————. 2007. *The World and Africa* and *Color and Democracy.* Edited by Henry Louis Gates. New York: Oxford University Press.

Durrani, Mariam. 2019. "Upsetting the Canon." *Anthropology News* 60, no. 2: e48–e52. DOI: 10.1111/AN.1134.

Eddy, Matthew Daniel. 2014. "How to See a Diagram: A Visual Anthropology of Chemical Affinity." *Osiris* 29, no. 1: 178–96. DOI: 10.1086/678093.

Eisenman, Peter. 2010. "Diagram: An Original Scene of Writing." In *The Diagrams of Architecture: AD Reader,* edited by Mark Garcia, 93–103. Chichester: Wiley.

Engelmann, Lukas, Caroline Humphrey, and Christos Lynteris. 2019. "Introduction: Diagrams beyond Mere Tools." *Social Analysis* 63, no. 4: 1–19. DOI: 10.3167/sa.2019.630401.

Evans-Pritchard, Edward E. 1940. *The Nuer: A Description of the Modes of Livelihood and Political Institutions of a Nilotic People.* Oxford: Oxford University Press.

Even-Ezra, Ayelet. 2021. *Lines of Thought: Branching Diagrams and the Medieval Mind.* Chicago: University of Chicago Press. DOI: 10.7208/chicago/9780226743110.001.0001.

Fabian, Johannes. 1990. "Presence and Representation: The Other and Anthropological Writing." *Critical Inquiry* 16, no. 4: 753–72. https://www.jstor.org/stable/1343766.

————. 2014. *Time and the Other: How Anthropology Makes Its Object.* New York: Columbia University Press.

Fanon, Frantz. 1963. *The Wretched of the Earth.* Translated by Constance Farrington. New York: Grove Press.

Firth, Raymond. 1939. *Primitive Polynesian Economy.* London: Routledge.

————. 1951. *Elements of Social Organization.* London: Watts.

Firth, Rosemary. 1943. *Housekeeping among Malay Peasants.* London: Taylor & Francis.

Gan, Elaine. 2021. "Diagrams: Making Multispecies Temporalities Visible." In *Experimenting with Ethnography: A Companion to Analysis,* edited by Andrea Ballestero and Brit Ross Winthereik, 106–20. Durham: Duke University Press. DOI: 10.1215/9781478013211-011.

Geertz, Clifford. 1973. *The Interpretation of Cultures: Selected Essays.* New York: Basic Books.

Geismar, Haidy. 2014. "Drawing It Out." *Visual Anthropology Review* 30, no. 2: 97–113. DOI: 10.1111/var.12041.

Gell, Alfred. 1998. *Art and Agency: An Anthropological Theory.* Oxford: Clarendon Press.

————. 1999. *The Art of Anthropology: Essays and Diagrams.* London: The Athlone Press.

Gibson, James J. 1986. *The Ecological Approach to Visual Perception.* New Tork: Taylor & Francis.

Giraldin, Odair. 2011. "Creating Affinity: Formal Friendship and Matrimonial Alliances among the Jê People and the Apinaje Case." *Vibrant: Virtual Brazilian Anthropology* 8, no. 2: 403–26. DOI: 10.1590/S1809-43412011000200018.

Gómez-Peña, Guillermo, and Lorena Rivero de Beer. 2009. "Guillermo Gómez-Peña: Ethno-Techno Politics." In *Interfaces of Performance,* edited by Maria Chatzichristodoulou, Janis Jefferies, and Rachel Zerihan, 141–52. Farnham: Ashgate.

Gordillo, Gastón. 2013. "The Void: Invisible Ruins on the Edges of Empire." In *Imperial Debris: On Ruins and Ruination,* edited by Ann Laura Stoler, 227–51. Durham: Duke University Press. DOI: 10.1215/9780822395850-008.

Graeber, David. 2007. *Lost People: Magic and the Legacy of Slavery in Madagascar.* Bloomington: Indiana University Press.

Gregory, Chris A. 2015. *Gifts and Commodities.* Chicago: HAU Books. https://haubooks.org/gifts-and-commodities/.

Grimshaw, Anna. 2001. *The Ethnographer's Eye: Ways of Seeing in Anthropology.* Cambridge: Cambridge University Press.

Grimshaw, Anna, and Keith Hart. 1995. "The Rise and Fall of Scientific Ethnography." In *The Future of Anthropology: Its*

Relevance to the Contemporary World, edited by Akbar S. Ahmed and Cris N. Shore, 46–64. London: Athlone.

Gupta, Akhil, and James Ferguson. 1998. "Discipline and Practice: 'The Field' as Site, Method, and Location in Anthropology." In *Anthropological Locations: Boundaries and Grounds of a Field Science,* edited by Akhil Gupta and James Ferguson, 1–46. Berkeley: University of California Press. DOI: 10.1525/9780520342392-002.

Hall, Stuart. 1986. "The Problem of Ideology: Marxism without Guarantees." *Journal of Communication Inquiry* 10, no. 2: 28–44. DOI: 10.1177/019685998601000203.

Hannabuss, Stuart. 2000. "Being There: Ethnographic Research and Autobiography." *Library Management* 21, no. 2: 99–107. DOI: 10.1108/01435120010309425.

Hardt, Michael, and Antonio Negri. 2009. *Commonwealth.* Cambridge: Harvard University Press.

Harrison, Faye V. 1988. "Introduction: An African Diaspora Perspective For Urban Anthropology." *Urban Anthropology and Studies of Cultural Systems and World Economic Development* 17, nos. 2–3: 111–41. https://www.jstor.org/stable/40553114.

———. 1997. "Anthropology as an Agent of Transformation: Introductory Comments and Queries." In *Decolonizing Anthropology: Moving Further toward an Anthropology for Liberation,* edited by Faye V. Harrison, 1–15. Arlington: Association of Black Anthropologists, American Anthropological Association.

Hastrup, Kirsten. 1990. "The Ethnographic Present: A Reinvention." *Cultural Anthropology* 5, no. 1: 45–61. https://www.jstor.org/stable/656503.

———. 2004. "Getting It Right: Knowledge and Evidence in Anthropology." *Anthropological Theory* 4, no. 4: 455–72. DOI: 10.1177/1463499604047921.

Herskovits, Melville Jean. 1952. *Economic Anthropology: A Study in Comparative Economics.* New York: Alfred Knopf.

Holbraad, Martin. 2012. *Truth in Motion: The Recursive Anthropology of Cuban Divination.* Chicago: University of Chicago Press.

hooks, bell. 1992. *Black Looks: Race and Representation.* Boston: South End Press.

Hurston, Zora Neale. 2018. *Barracoon: The Story of the Last "Black Cargo."* Edited by Deborah G. Plant. New York: Amistad.

Ingold, Tim. 2000. *The Perception of the Environment: Essays on Livelihood, Dwelling and Skill.* London: Routledge.

———. 2007. *Lines: A Brief History.* London: Routledge.

Jablonko, Allison, and Maurice Godelier. 1983. "Elements of Baruya Ethnography: Trade." http://jablonko-baruya. pacific-credo.fr/bgBbottom.html.

Jackson, Michael. 1996. "Introduction: Phenomenology, Radical Empiricism, and Anthropological Critique." In *Things as They Are: New Directions in Phenomenological Anthropology,* edited by Michael Jackson, 1–50. Bloomington: Indiana University Press.

Jackson, Phyllis J. 2002. "Liberating Blackness and Interrogating Whiteness." In *Art/Women/California 1950–2000: Parallels and Intersections,* edited by Diana Burgess Fuller, Daniela Salvioni, Gail Tsukiyama, and Deborah Munk, 59–78. Berkeley: University of California Press.

Jameson, Frederic. 1974. *The Prison-House of Language: A Critical Account of Structuralism and Russian Formalism.* Princeton: Princeton University Press.

———. 1981. *The Political Unconscious: Narrative as a Socially Symbolic Act.* Ithaca: Cornell University Press.

Jegathesan, Mythri. 2021. "Black Feminist Plots before the Plantationocene and Anthropology's 'Regional Closets.'" *Feminist Anthropology* 2, no. 1: 78–93. DOI: 10.1002/ fea2.12037.

Jobson, Ryan Cecil. 2020. "The Case for Letting Anthropology Burn: Sociocultural Anthropology in 2019." *American Anthropologist* 122, no. 2: 259–71. DOI: 10.1111/aman.13398.

Kelly, Ann. 2012. "The Progress of the Project: Scientific Traction in the Gambia." In *Differentiating Development: Beyond an Anthropology of Critique,* edited by Soumhya Venkatesan and Thomas Yarrow, 65–83. New York: Berghahn Books. DOI: 10.1515/9780857453044-006.

Kluckhohn, Clyde Kay Maben. 1949. "The Philosophy of the Navajo Indians." In *Ideological Differences and World Order: Studies in the Philosophy and Science of the World's Cultures,* edited by Filmer Stuart Cuckow Northrop, 356–84. New Haven: Yale University Press.

Knoespel, Kenneth J. 2001. "Diagrams as Piloting Devices in the Philosophy of Gilles Deleuze." *Théorie, Littérature, Enseignement* no. 19 (Automne): 145–65. https://www.puv-editions.fr/ouvrage/deleuze-chantier/.

Krämer, Sybille. 2010. "'Epistemology of the Line': Reflections on the Diagrammatical Mind." In *Studies in Diagrammatology and Diagram Praxis,* edited by Olga Pombo and Alexander Gerner, 13–38. London: College Publications.

Lambek, Michael. 2010. "Toward an Ethics of the Act." In *Ordinary Ethics: Anthropology, Language, and Action,* edited by Michael Lambek, 39–63. New York: Fordham University Press. https://www.jstor.org/stable/j.ctt13x07p9.6.

Langdon Roche, Emma. 1914. *Historic Sketches of the South.* New York: The Knickerbocker Press.

Latour, Bruno. 1986. "Visualisation and Cognition: Drawing Things Together." In *Knowledge and Society — Studies in the Sociology of Culture Past and Present,* Vol. 6, edited by Elizabeth Long and Henrika Kuklick, 1–40. Greenwich: JAI Press. http://www.bruno-latour.fr/sites/default/files/21-DRAWING-THINGS-TOGETHER-GB.pdf.

———. 1993. *We Have Never Been Modern.* Translated by Catherine Porter. Cambridge: Harvard University Press.

Law, John, and Marianne Lien. 2018. "Denaturalizing Nature." In *A World of Many Worlds,* edited by Marisol de la Cadena and Mario Blaser, 131–71. Durham: Duke University Press. DOI: 10.2307/j.ctv125jpzq.9.

Layard, John. 1936. "Maze-Dances and the Ritual of the Labyrinth in Malekula." *Folklore* 47, no. 2: 123–70. DOI: 10.1080/0015587X.1936.9718634.

Lazar, Sian. 2014. "Historical Narrative, Mundane Political Time, and Revolutionary Moments: Coexisting Temporalities in the Lived Experience of Social Movements." *Journal of the Royal Anthropological Institute* 20, S1: 91–108. DOI: 10.1111/1467-9655.12095.

Lenhard, Johannes, and Farhan Samanani. 2020. "Introduction: Ethnography, Dwelling and Home-Making." In *Home: Ethnographic Encounters,* edited by Johannes Lenhard and Farhan Samanani, 1–29. London: Bloomsbury Academic.

Lévi-Strauss, Claude. 1966. *The Savage Mind.* Translated by George Weidenfeld. London: Weidenfeld and Nicolson.

———. 1969. *The Elementary Structures of Kinship.* Translated by James Harle Bell and John Richard von Sturmer. Boston: Beacon Press.

Liboiron, Max. 2021. *Pollution Is Colonialism.* Durham: Duke University Press.

Llobera, Josep R. 1976. "The History of Anthropology as a Problem." *Critique of Anthropology* 2, no. 7: 17–42. DOI: 10.1177/0308275X7600200703.

Lynch, Michael. 1991. "Pictures of Nothing? Visual Construals in Social Theory." *Sociological Theory* 9, no. 1: 1–21. DOI: 10.2307/201870.

Lynteris, Christos. 2017. "Zoonotic Diagrams: Mastering and Unsettling Human-Animal Relations: Zoonotic Diagrams." *Journal of the Royal Anthropological Institute* 23, no. 3 (September): 463–85. DOI: 10.1111/1467-9655.12649.

Maguire, Patricia. 1987. *Doing Participatory Research: A Feminist Approach.* Amherst: Center for International Education, University of Massachusetts.

Malinowski, Bronislaw. 1922. *Argonauts of the Western Pacific: An Account of Native Enterprise and Adventure in the Archipelagoes of Melanesian New Guinea.* London: Routledge.

Manning, Erin. 2019. "Experimenting Immediation: Collaboration and the Politics of Fabulation." In *Immediation II,* edited by Erin Manning, Anna Munster, and Bodil M.S. Thomsen, 361–95. London: Open Humanities Press.

Marriott, McKim. 1989. "Constructing an Indian Ethnosociology." *Contributions to Indian Sociology* 23, no. 1: 1–39. DOI: 10.1177/006996689023001003.

Massumi, Brian. 1992. *A User's Guide to Capitalism and Schizophrenia: Deviations from Deleuze and Guattari.* Cambridge: MIT Press.

———. 1998. "The Diagram as Technique of Existence." *ANY: Architecture New York* 23: 42–47. https://www.jstor.org/stable/41856102.

———. 2011. *Semblance and Event: Activist Philosophy and the Occurrent Arts.* Cambridge: MIT Press.

Miller, Carolyn R. 1992. "Kairos in the Rhetoric of Science." In *A Rhetoric of Doing: Essays on Written Discourse in Honor of James L. Kinneavy,* edited by Stephen P. Witte, Neil Nakadate, and Roger Dennis Cherry, 310–27. Carbondale: Southern Illinois University Press.

Miller, Mitchell. n.d. "Red Road Dialectograms: Drawing of the Niven's Flat." *Red Road Flats.* https://www.redroadflats.org.uk/page_id_2090/.

Mimica, Jadran. 1988. *Intimations of Infinity: The Cultural Meanings of the Iqwaye Counting and Number Systems.* New York: St. Martin's Press.

Minh-ha, Trinh T. 1991. *When the Moon Waxes Red: Representation, Gender, and Cultural Politics.* New York: Routledge.

Morgan, Lewis Henry. 1871. *Systems of Consanguinity and Affinity of the Human Family.* Washington, DC: Smithsonian Institution.

Mosse, David. 2006. "Anti-Social Anthropology? Objectivity, Objection, and the Ethnography of Public Policy and Professional Communities." *Journal of the Royal*

Anthropological Institute 12, no. 4: 935–56. DOI: 10.1111/j.1467-9655.2006.00371.x.

Munn, Nancy D. 1986. *The Fame of Gawa: A Symbolic Study of Value Transformation in a Massim (Papua New Guinea) Society.* Cambridge: Cambridge University Press.

Nash, June C. 2007. "When Isms Become Wasms: Paradigms Lost and Regained." In *Practicing Ethnography in a Globalizing World: An Anthropological Odyssey,* 15–34. Lanham: AltaMira Press.

Neich, Roger. 1993. *Painted Histories: Early Maori Figurative Painting.* Auckland: Auckland University Press.

Oliver, Douglas L. 1955. *A Solomon Island Society: Kinship and Leadership Among the Siuai of Bougainville.* Cambridge: Harvard University Press.

Oliver, Mary. 2008. *Red Bird: Poems.* Boston: Beacon Press.

Ó Maoilearca, John. 2006. *Post-Continental Philosophy: An Outline.* London: Continuum.

Osborn, J.R. 2005. "Theory Pictures as Trails: Diagrams and the Navigation of Theoretical Narratives." *Cognitive Science Online* 3, no. 2: 15–44. https://cogsci-online.ucsd.edu/3/3-4.pdf.

Parkin, David. 2000. "Templates, Evocations, and the Long-Term Fieldworker." In *Anthropologists in a Wider World: Essays on Field Research,* edited by Paul Dresch, Wendy James, and David Parkin, 91–108. New York: Berghahn Books. DOI: 10.2307/j.ctv287sdrb.10.

Partridge, Tristan. 2014. "Diagrams in Anthropology: Lines and Interactions." *Life Off the Grid.* https://anthropologyoffthegrid.wordpress.com/ethnograms/diagrams-in-anthropology/.

———. 2015. "Recoupling Groups Who Resist: Dimensions of Difference, Opposition and Affirmation." *Journal of Resistance Studies* 1, no. 2: 12–50. https://resistance-journal.org/wp-content/uploads/2016/01/Issue-2-Article-1.pdf.

———. 2025. "Grid." In *International Handbook of Visual Research Methods in Anthropology* edited by Rupert Cox and Chris Wright. London: Routledge.

Pasternak, Shiri, Hayden King, and Riley Yesno. 2019. *Land Back: A Yellowhead Institute Red Paper.* Winnipeg: Yellow Head Institute. https://redpaper.yellowheadinstitute.org/wp-content/uploads/2019/10/red-paper-report-final.pdf.

Peirce, Charles S. 1931. *Collected Papers of Charles Sanders Peirce.* Edited by Charles Hartshorne and Paul Weiss. Cambridge: Harvard University Press.

Reid, Colleen. 2004. "Advancing Women's Social Justice Agendas: A Feminist Action Research Framework." *International Journal of Qualitative Methods* 3, no. 3: 1–15. DOI: 10.1177/160940690400300301.

Rio, Knut. 2005. "Discussions around a Sand-Drawing: Creations of Agency and Society in Melanesia." *Journal of the Royal Anthropological Institute* 11, no. 3: 401–23. DOI: 10.1111/j.1467-9655.2005.00243.x.

Rivers, William H.R. 1910. "The Genealogical Method of Anthropological Inquiry." *The Sociological Review* a3, no. 1: 1–12. DOI: 10.1111/j.1467-954X.1910.tb02078.x.

Rosa, Jonathan, and Yarimar Bonilla. 2017. "Deprovincializing Trump, Decolonizing Diversity, and Unsettling Anthropology." *American Ethnologist* 44, no. 2 (May): 201–8. DOI: 10.1111/amet.12468.

Rose, Deborah Bird. 2000. *Dingo Makes Us Human: Life and Land in an Australian Aboriginal Culture.* Cambridge: Cambridge University Press.

Ruppert, Evelyn. 2016. "A Baroque Sensibility for Big Data Visualisations." In *Modes of Knowing: Resources from the Baroque,* edited by John Law and Evelyn Sharon Rupert, 136–61. Manchester: Mattering Press.

Sahlins, Marshall. 1972. *Stone Age Economics.* Chicago: Aldine-Atherton.

Sanjek, Roger. 1991. "The Ethnographic Present." *Man* 26, no. 4: 609–28. DOI: 10.2307/2803772.

Seremetakis, C. Nadia. 1993. "The Memory of the Senses: Historical Perception, Commensal Exchange, and Modernity." *Visual Anthropology Review* 9, no. 2: 2–18. DOI: 10.1525/var.1993.9.2.2.

Simpson, Audra. 2014. *Mohawk Interruptus: Political Life Across the Borders of Settler States.* Durham: Duke University Press.

Simpson, Bob. 2006. "'You Don't Do Fieldwork, Fieldwork Does You': Between Subjectivation and Objectivation in Anthropological Fieldwork." In *The SAGE Handbook of Fieldwork,* edited by Dick Hobbs, and Richard Wright, 125–37. London: SAGE. DOI: 10.4135/9781848608085.

Singh, Bhrigupati, and Jane I. Guyer. 2016. "A Joyful History of Anthropology." *HAU: Journal of Ethnographic Theory* 6, no. 2: 197–211. DOI: 10.14318/hau6.2.014.

Smith, Linda Tuhiwai. 1999. *Decolonizing Methodologies: Research and Indigenous Peoples.* London: Zed Books.

Springgay, Stephanie, and Zofia Zaliwska. 2015. "Diagrams and Cuts: A Materialist Approach to Research-Creation." *Cultural Studies ↔ Critical Methodologies* 15, no. 2: 136–44. DOI: 10.1177/1532708614562881.

Stocking, George W. 1992. "The Ethnographer's Magic: Fieldwork in British Anthropology from Tylor to Malinowski." In *The Ethnographer's Magic and Other Essays in the History of Anthropology,* 12–59. Madison: University of Wisconsin Press.

Stoler, Ann Laura. 2008. "Imperial Debris: Reflections on Ruins and Ruination." *Cultural Anthropology* 23, no. 2: 191–219. https://www.jstor.org/stable/20484502.

Stoller, Paul. 1992. "Artaud, Rouch, and the Cinema of Cruelty." *Visual Anthropology Review* 8, no. 2: 50–57. DOI: 10.1525/var.1992.8.2.50.

Stone, Allucquere Rosanne. 2002. "The Baby or the Bath Water; Being an Inquiry into the Nature of Woman, Womyn, Art, Time, and Timing in Five Thousand Words or Less." In *Art/Women/California 1950–2000: Parallels and Intersections,* edited by Diana Burgess Fuller, Daniela Salvioni, Gail Tsukiyama, and Deborah Munk, 335–47. Berkeley: University of California Press.

Strathern, Marilyn. 1988. *The Gender of the Gift: Problems with Women and Problems with Society in Melanesia.* Berkeley: University of California Press.

———. 2005. *Kinship, Law and the Unexpected: Relatives Are Always a Surprise*. New York: Cambridge University Press.

Taylor, Lucien, ed. 1994. *Visualizing Theory: Selected Essays from VAR, 1990–1994*. London: Routledge.

Thorkelson, Eli. 2016. "The Infinite Rounds of the Stubborn: Reparative Futures at a French Political Protest." *Cultural Anthropology* 31, no. 4: 493–519. DOI: 10.14506/ca31.4.03.

Trouillot, Michel-Rolph. 2003. *Global Transformations: Anthropology and the Modern World*. New York: Palgrave. DOI: 10.1007/978-1-137-04144-9.

Tuck, Eve, and K. Wayne Yang. 2012. "Decolonization Is Not a Metaphor." *Decolonization: Indigeneity, Education and Society* 1, no. 1: 1–40. https://jps.library.utoronto.ca/index.php/des/article/view/18630/15554.

Turner, Victor W. 1985. *On the Edge of the Bush: Anthropology as Experience*. Edited by Edith L.B. Turner. Tucson: University of Arizona Press.

Tyson, Charlie. 2019. "Apocalypse Chic." *Chronicle of Higher Education,* August 22. https://www.chronicle.com/interactives/20190823-tyson-fatalism.

Wagner, Roy. 1986. *Symbols That Stand for Themselves*. Chicago: University of Chicago Press.

Watson, Arthur. 1934. *The Early Iconography of the Tree of Jesse*. London: Oxford University Press.

Watson, Janell. 2009. *Guattari's Diagrammatic Thought: Writing between Lacan and Deleuze*. London: Continuum.

Whitehead, Alfred North. 1967. *Science and the Modern World*. New York: Free Press.

Widlok, Thomas. 2013. "Sharing: Allowing Others to Take What Is Valued." *HAU: Journal of Ethnographic Theory* 3, no. 2 (Summer): 11–31. DOI: 10.14318/hau3.2.003.

Young, J.L. 1919. "The Paumotu Conception of the Heavens and of Creation." *The Journal of the Polynesian Society* 28, no. 4: 209–11. https://www.jstor.org/stable/20701751.

Zdebik, Jakub. 2012. *Deleuze and the Diagram: Aesthetic Threads in Visual Organization*. London: Continuum.

www.ingramcontent.com/pod-product-compliance
Lightning Source LLC
Chambersburg PA
CBHW050649270326
41927CB00012B/2949